Alma Schwabe and Arlene Lee

MINIQUILTS

TAFELBERG

To our husbands for their
understanding and encouragement

© 1990 Tafelberg Publishers Limited
28 Wale Street, Cape Town 8001

Translated by H. Gericke
Photography by David Briers
Styling by Danny Boschi

Illustrations by Peter Ebsworth
Wooden items by Wolf Schwabe
Cover design and typography by G&G Design
Set in 10 on 12 pt Plantin by Diatype Setting

Printed and bound by National Book Printers,
Goodwood, Cape

First edition, first impression 1990

ISBN 0 624 02950 6

Contents

Before you begin...

Making miniquilts, whether to display in your home or to sell, is becoming immensely popular. These miniature quilts are something very special – an irresistible challenge to any needlewoman, and particularly to quilting and patchwork enthusiasts, homemakers and even toy collectors.

Time has become a luxury, and miniquilts offer an opportunity to satisfy one's creative urge, experiment with new techniques and in a short time produce a unique article to display with pride.

Patchwork is an art form that dates back several centuries. Young girls in Colonial America were taught sewing techniques through quiltmaking. As a girl's skill increased, her quilts became more complicated. Traditionally, a young girl made twelve quilts. During her engagement period, she used all the skills she had acquired to design and make her thirteenth quilt – her masterpiece. Today, the inexperienced needlewoman can apply the same principle. By starting with a basic design, she can gradually develop knowledge, experience and expertise in selecting fabric, putting together colour combinations and applying sewing techniques.

One often hears the question: "A miniquilt is fine, but what do you *use* it for?" or "Why bother with small patchwork when you might just as well make a large quilt?"

The time and cost involved in making a large quilt is enough reason for working on a small scale. We are all pressed for time – we work all day, drive children around, do shopping, cook . . . Once we have set aside time for the family, there is hardly any time left for hobbies. Considering that it usually takes about six months to complete a large quilt, I am sure you will agree that a miniquilt is indeed the solution. There are patchwork enthusiasts who are happy to produce only one or two quilts a year, but many others would like to complete more items in order to experiment with different colours and techniques and to enjoy the satisfaction of having created something beautiful and unique.

With so many designs and patterns available, it is amazingly simple to make a miniquilt. You may feel free, however, to use more complicated and advanced patterns to create real works of art.

Most of the miniature quilts in this book can be completed within a day, and do not require metres of fabric. Most needlewomen have enough fabric remnants to keep them occupied for many years in completing dozens of miniquilts.

A miniature quilt in the making can easily be taken along wherever you go, and you can spend your time profitably while watching your child's rugby match or waiting in the doctor's waiting room, where your diligence might even inspire your fellow patients!

Once you have completed a few miniquilts, you will feel more confident when you do attempt a large quilt. A large quilt will no longer appear such a daunting and time-consuming project. You will soon find that making miniquilts is as addictive as eating peanuts – you always want to have just one more.

Other advantages of miniquilts are that they are so much easier to handle, they allow practice in quilting and give you the opportunity to experiment with colour, design and sewing techniques. Your own imagination and creativity will amaze you, and you will hardly be able to believe that you have made something so beautiful yourself.

Miniquilts have many uses. They are equally effective as wall-hangings, on shelves (with a stand), as fire screens, and even in the bathroom or over the backs or armrests of armchairs and couches. A miniquilt on the coffee table in the lounge will make an excellent conversation piece. Framed or mounted behind glass, a miniquilt becomes a real work of art (p. 42). A miniquilt on the front of a dress or on children's clothes will certainly catch the eye. A slightly bigger miniquilt makes a very special pram cover or cot quilt. It is an ideal cover for a doll's bed. Your much worn miniquilt may become a treasured heirloom. Imagine your grandchildren quarrelling over whose turn it is to play with Grandma's old doll's blanket!

A miniquilt is a thing of beauty which satisfies the creative urge of today's woman. You do not need to be an experienced needlewoman – even if it takes you *two* days to complete your first miniquilt, accept the challenge and go for it!

Finally, should anyone dare ask you why you are making a miniquilt, simply ask: "Why not?"

Materials

It is a good idea to buy and gather everything you need for your quilting project (if you do not have it conveniently at hand) and store it in an attractive basket – ready for use when the urge takes you.

Fabrics

The word "patchwork" can be misleading, as one rarely has enough remnants to complete a large quilt, and is therefore forced to do some shopping. However, most of the miniquilts in this book require very little fabric and needlewomen should be able to complete most of them from their collection of fabric oddments. Do have another look at that bag of remnants from children's clothes, curtains, etc. for fabrics of the colour and texture that you need. Your completed project will bring back many happy memories.

When buying fabric, bear in mind the following guidelines:

☐ Choose the best quality you can afford.

☐ Buy only pure cotton. It is more durable and easier to handle than mixtures or fabrics such as silk and synthetics.

☐ Quantities calculated in this book are for 115 cm wide fabrics.

☐ Colour combinations are very important. Combine light and dark colours for contrast. In a large project, different shades of the same colour may be used. In a smaller article, however, a more distinctive contrast is needed to be really effective. You may like to use the photographs in the book as a guide to work out your own colour combinations.

☐ The design on print fabrics, for example flowers or spots, should be very small. Too bold a design draws attention away from the small patches, with the result that much of the intended effect is lost.

☐ It might be a good idea to start off by experimenting with a sample. Cut off small pieces of the fabrics you intend using, arrange them together and decide whether the effect pleases you. Examine your sample from a distance, or pin the bits of fabric to a curtain to see if the colours can be distinguished clearly.

☐ It is preferable to wash all fabrics beforehand. Wash dark colours that might run separately. To test a fabric for colourfastness, wash it in a solution of 3 parts cold water mixed with 1 part white vinegar. It is not advisable to use fabrics that run – even after this treatment. Of course, this does not apply to an article that you never intend washing. Unwashed fabrics are easier to cut and also look better.

☐ What goes inside a quilt is almost as important as the top. Soft, thin batting will give the best results. Do not use thick batting, it will give the quilt a puffy effect. Needle-punch or thin, fluffy fabrics, such as flannelette (old nappies), give good results.

Equipment

You do not need special equipment for making miniquilts, and you probably have most of the items mentioned below:

☐ *Beeswax* Run quilting or machine thread through beeswax. This will make it easier to pull through three layers of fabric and prevent knotting when quilting.

☐ *Cardboard or hard plastic* For certain projects you will need firm templates to trace the outlines of triangles, squares, and other shapes. Old X-ray films make good templates.

☐ *Coloured pencils* A light-coloured pencil will leave a clear mark on a dark fabric and vice versa. This is particularly handy for cutting patches of different sizes.

☐ *Embroidery frame* A frame is very useful for quilting, appliqué and embroidery. A round frame gives the best results. It enables you to stretch the fabric (even the three layers of a quilt) and to keep it taut, which will ensure that the final product is smoothly and evenly quilted.

☐ *Glue stick (Pritt)* For some projects, you will need a glue stick to paste the pieces of a design, for example, *Christmas decorations* (instructions on p. 64-66).

☐ *Iron* You need an iron (preferably a steam iron) to iron fabrics before you start working and to press seams.

☐ *Needles* You will need a variety of needles – long ones for basting and embroidery, and short ones for appliquéing and quilting.

☐ *Pencils* An ordinary pencil will do for tracing quilting patterns onto fabric.

☐ *Pins* Use the best quality available, preferably long thin ones with large heads. Avoid pins that are thick, blunt or rusty.

☐ *Rotary cutter and board* Once you have seen how quickly and accurately these tools work, you will find them indispensable. You can cut up to ten layers at a time. The knife with the biggest blade gives the best results. The plastic board has been designed in such a way that it cannot be damaged by the cutter.

☐ *Ruler (to use with rotary cutter and board)* An ordinary, thick, transparent plastic ruler will do for use with a rotary cutter and board. The clear marks make it very easy to cut small strips. Some sewing shops sell wider and longer transparent rulers for this purpose.

☐ *Scissors* You will need three pairs of scissors: a large, sharp pair of fabric scissors, a pair for cutting paper and a pair of embroidery scissors for small jobs such as cutting thread and trimming seam allowances.

☐ *Seam ripper* This is an indispensable tool for unpicking machine stitching.

☐ *Spray starch* Small pieces of fabric are easier to handle and less likely to fray if you spray them with starch.

☐ *Tape measure* Measure fabrics and remnants with a tape measure to determine whether you have sufficient for a particular project.

☐ *Thimble* A thimble is essential, especially for quilting. Different types are available, for example metal and leather. Most quilters use a leather thimble on the third finger of the right hand.

☐ *Thread* Use 100% cotton thread for quilting or the imported quilting thread sold by specialist shops. Choose a colour that blends with your darkest fabric. If, however, you are using a large variety of fabrics as, for example, in *Flower garden* (photograph on p. 23), a neutral colour will be best. Matching polyester thread works well for machine stitching.

☐ *Water-soluble pen* This is handy for tracing quilting patterns onto fabrics. It is optional, since an ordinary pencil works just as well.

Note Always wash articles thoroughly when completed as the chemicals in some pens may cause irreversible damage: stains may form and, even worse, small holes can appear in your work.

Techniques

Patchwork allows for so many variations that no one has to use the same technique twice. The principal technique illustrated in this book is the quick-cut, quick-stitch method, using a pair of scissors or a rotary cutter. See *Furrows in the field* (p. 34-35), *Twenty-four stars* (p. 35-38), *Star log cabin* (p. 38-41) and *Lightning* (p. 41-43).

Cutting the fabric

The instructions given below explain how to cut fabrics in the conventional way with a pair of scissors, as well as the quick-cut, quick-stitch method. Follow the step-by-step instructions to save a lot of time and achieve great satisfaction.

How to cut several layers of fabric at a time with a pair of scissors

Use a very sharp pair of scissors and cut through all the layers. Do not try to cut through more than five layers simultaneously.

☐ Trace the outline of the template onto the reverse side of one of the pieces of fabric with an ordinary pencil.

☐ Place the layers of fabric on the ironing board one at a time and iron each layer before adding the next one to the pile. Match the edges and grain of the fabrics wherever possible. Place the marked piece of fabric right on top.

Hint Spray starch between the layers to keep them from slipping.

☐ Pin the layers together between each set of marks to make sure that the layers of fabric do not move.

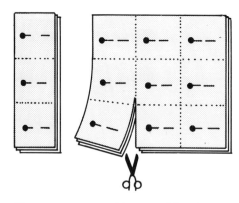

How to cut several layers of fabric at a time with a rotary cutter

The quick-cut, quick-stitch method using a rotary cutter is fast gaining popularity. It is not surprising, as it is the fastest and most accurate way of cutting fabric, especially strips. The blade of the scissors lifts the fabric, and with the rotary cutter this does not happen. Start off by cutting only a few (two or three) layers together until you have mastered the technique.

☐ Trim the selvages of the fabric before you start.

☐ Fold the fabric lengthwise with right sides facing and raw edges neatly together.

☐ Use the lines on the ruler to cut the required widths, or measure and mark the fabric as usual.

☐ Place a set-square or a second ruler exactly on the fold of the fabric and firmly against the plastic ruler.

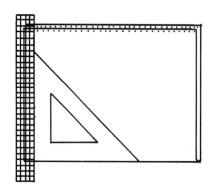

☐ Remove the set-square (or second ruler) without moving the ruler.

☐ Press hard on the blade of the rotary cutter in a downward and horizontal direction, moving away from your body. This is very important, or you may cut yourself. In this way you will cut a neat, straight edge.

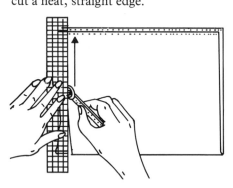

☐ Cut the strips into squares if required by the project.

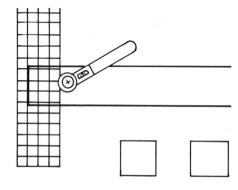

Hint To save even more of your precious time, use the rotary cutter and cut vertical strips which have been sewn together. Place your ruler on the pressed strips that have been joined and cut off squares of the required size (see diagram at the top of p. 5). To ensure greater accuracy it is better in this instance to cut only one layer at a time.

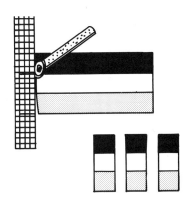

You can fold the fabric over twice to give four layers and then cut it. The cut edges will still fit perfectly.

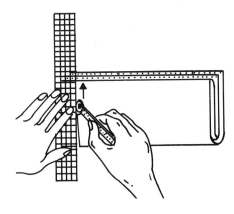

When the strip you have cut is folded open, it should be straight, and not curved in the middle. Therefore it is important to keep the ruler at a 90° angle with the folded edge.

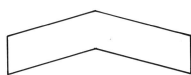

Sewing the fabric

You may find the following hints useful, as most of the projects require some machine-sewing:
☐ Set your machine at 10-12 stitches per 2,5 cm.
☐ Pin the patches together with right sides facing and feed them through the machine.
☐ Leave a seam allowance of 6 mm in patchwork. Many presser feet are exactly 6 mm wide, providing a useful

guide. Alternatively, mark your sewing machine by using a strip of adhesive tape or masking tape.
☐ Pull the upper as well as the lower threads back and hold them there when you start stitching to prevent them from being drawn into the machine and knotting.

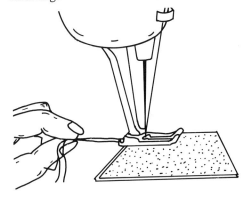

☐ When you are stitching, be careful to remove the pins as they approach the needle. If you stitch over them, you may damage the needle and the fabric.

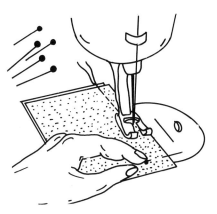

☐ Where two seams join, make sure that they lie in different directions, or the seam will be too thick and the corners will not match.

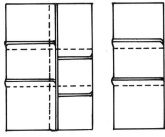

☐ To save time and thread, stitch patches in succession without cutting the thread between them. When all the patches have been stitched, cut the

threads between them and press the patches.

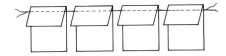

☐ Undo stitching errors with a seam ripper. Never try to tear patches apart. Use the seam ripper and slash a stitch every 13 mm. Turn the patch over and pull the thread in the opposite direction – it should come undone quite easily. Remove all the bits of loose thread before stitching any further.

Hand-piecing

☐ Mark the seamline on the reverse side of the patch.
☐ Begin with a back stitch and baste from one corner to the next – try to sew about 5 stitches per 2,5 cm.
☐ Where two patches meet, simply push the needle through to the other side and continue sewing – do not sew over the seam.

Appliqué

Appliqué is a method where a small piece of fabric is sewn onto a larger piece. It can be done by hand or by machine. See, for example, *Charms* p. (46), *Nine hearts* (p. 46-47), *Fanned heart* (p. 47-49) and *Scottish terriers* (p. 52-53).

Hand appliqué
☐ Make a plastic or cardboard template of the appliqué design.
☐ Place the template on the right side of the fabric, trace around the outline of the template with a pencil, and cut out.
Note If there is no seam allowance on the template, cut about 3 mm outside the pencil line.
☐ Clip curves almost as far as the pencil line. (The edge will be folded in on the pencil line later.)
☐ Place the reverse side of the piece to be appliquéd onto the right side of the background fabric and pin.

☐ Using thread of the same colour as the appliqué piece, sew along the pencil line with small invisible stitches. Tuck the edge under the appliqué piece, either with your fingertips or with the needle as you go.

Hints
☐ Appliqué patches can also be basted to the background with small stitches 3 mm from the folded edge, or with blanket stitch around the raw edges, using thread in a contrasting colour (see *Kittens*, p. 14).
☐ For a smoother and more even finish, use an embroidery frame.

Machine appliqué
☐ Make a cardboard or plastic template of the appliqué design.
☐ Place the template on the right side of the fabric and trace the outline with a pencil.
☐ Cut out along the pencil line and pin or baste to the background.
Note No seam allowance is needed.
☐ Use iron-on interfacing on the reverse side of the appliqué to make it easier to handle and to prevent fraying. Spray-on starch may also be used.
☐ Use thread in the same colour as the appliqué patch and stitch along the edge with ordinary stitching to eliminate unsightly folds and wrinkles later on.
☐ Set your sewing machine on satin stitch. Normally the stitch width is 3 mm, but the exact width depends on the type of fabric and the size of the appliqué patch. An embroidery foot is very useful, because you have a better view of what you are doing. Always practise on a fabric scrap first.
☐ Stitch carefully along the edge, making sure that the needle enters the appliqué patch and the background fabric alternately.
☐ Carefully guide the fabric around the corners and make sure that you stitch evenly to prevent puckering. If you pull the fabric gently with your left hand as it moves out from under the foot while you are stitching, you will sew more evenly.
☐ When you reach a corner, leave the needle in the fabric in the down position. Lift the presser foot, turn the article to the position you need to continue stitching, lower the presser foot and sew.

Pressing

For a professional effect, try the following:
☐ A steam iron is preferable.
☐ Press small pieces of patchwork on the right side. In this way you will get the small seams to lie flat more easily.

☐ In the case of light-coloured patches, place them on the ironing board reverse side down and press the seam towards the darker patch. The seam will not show on the right side.

☐ When ironing, simply press down lightly instead of moving the iron to and fro. To-and-fro movements may stretch the fabric, and you may end up with sides that are longer than intended.

Layers

☐ Cut the backing of the quilt 10 cm wider than the top all round. The backing may be joined if necessary.
☐ Cut thin batting the exact size of the backing.
☐ Place the backing right side down on a clean table or on the floor. Place the batting over the backing. Smooth the two layers. Place the top section over these two layers. The 10 cm of excess width on the two bottom layers will extend right round the edges.

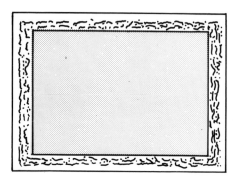

☐ Baste the three layers together – start in the centre and sew large stitches toward the sides and corners. Do not end off the basting stitches so that you will be able to smooth out any un-evenness in the fabric towards the edges.
Hint Instead of basting use safety pins through all 3 layers every 10 cm.

Quilting

It is amazing how quilting stitches, which are nothing more than small basting stitches, can add depth and dimension to a piece of patchwork.

Preparation
☐ Remove all loose threads and cut thread ends close to the completed article.
☐ Check seam allowances on the wrong side of the quilting and trim all excess fabric.
☐ Press the completed article thoroughly, first on the reverse side and then on the right side. Remember that this is your last chance to press the article well and to correct mistakes.
☐ If you want a quilt pattern, make a cardboard or plastic template and with a soft pencil trace it lightly onto the right side of the fabric. There is no need for marking if you are going to quilt on or close to the stitching lines.

The quilting process
Quilting can be done with or without a frame. The advantage of using a frame

is that the article is stretched smoothly and unevenness can be almost completely eliminated. Quilting a very small miniquilt will be easier without a frame.

☐ Use the smallest needle that you find comfortable to work with, and ordinary fabric thread (single thread) if you are unable to find quilting thread.

☐ Run the thread through beeswax to prevent tangling (optional).

☐ Give the end of the thread a single knot.

☐ From above, push the needle between the batting and the top layer and draw the thread through to leave the knot lodged between the two layers.

Note Wear a thimble (leather or metal) on the third finger of your right hand.

☐ Push the needle straight down, and push it back upwards when you feel the point with your left hand. Try to sew small, evenly spaced stitches. As you become more skilled, you will develop a rhythmic movement, and eventually you will be able to have up to five stitches on your needle.

☐ To end a line of stitching, make a single small knot in the thread and pull the needle through the layers of fabric and batting, leaving the knot lodged between the layers.

Finishing

Finishing a miniquilt with a border and/or binding is almost as important as all the previous steps. On a very small article it is sometimes advisable to use a dark colour for the border.

Borders

It is important to measure the edges very accurately to get your quilt exactly symmetrical. Because stretching often occurs during stitching, you may find that two opposite edges are not the same length. If this is the case, do the following:

☐ Take a measurement right in the centre of the quilt from left to right, and also from top to bottom. Make a note of these measurements, and calculate the average length of the sides.

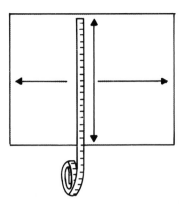

☐ Cut two strips according to the length of the horizontal edges. Fold the quilt, as well as the two strips, in half.

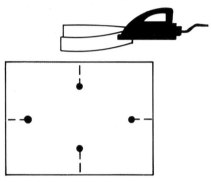

☐ Pin the centre of the quilt to the centre of each strip of fabric with right sides together.

☐ Pin the rest of each strip to the edge of the quilt, making sure that the ends extend exactly to the ends of the horizontal edges of the quilt. Stitch.

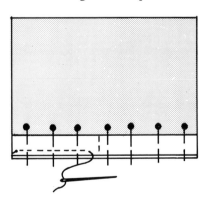

☐ Repeat with the vertical sides.

Note Whether you first do the horizontal and then the vertical sides or vice versa makes no difference.

Binding

The binding may be cut on the bias or along the grain of the fabric. Binding on the bias is better for neat corners.

☐ Cut a binding of ± 5 cm wide. To calculate the length, add ± 10 cm all round (to allow for the corners and for joining the ends).

Note If you do not have sufficient fabric, join the strips.

☐ Fold the strip lengthwise down the middle with reverse sides together and press the fold.

☐ Beginning in the middle of one of the vertical sides of the quilt, place the strip on the edge of the quilt, with the raw edges of the strip and the quilt together. Begin ± 1,5 cm from the end of the strip and stitch along the edge as far as ± 6 mm from the first corner.

Hint Use a slightly larger stitch than before, as the layers that have to pass under the presser foot are quite thick.

☐ When the needle is 6 mm from the edge of the quilt, lift it out of the fabric and the batting.

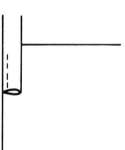

☐ Fold the binding as shown below, making sure that the fold lies exactly on the raw edge. Pin.

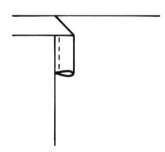

☐ Fold the binding back towards the other edge. On the right side a line will be formed at 45° to the corner (diagram on p. 8).

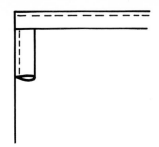

☐ While it remains under the machine, turn the quilt in the new direction, lift the needle from the work to clear the fold. Stitch a 6 mm seam from the edge of the quilt to the next corner. Make another fold and continue as described above up to ± 1,5 cm from the starting point.

☐ Stitch the two ends of the binding together. Trim excess fabric and stitch the last bit of binding onto the quilt and across the seam (folded open). *Note* Some projects require a different finishing method, for example the *Rainbow* (p. 18-19), the *Four-block quilt* (p. 29) and the *Yo-yo* (p. 15).

Projects

The purpose of the different projects is especially to teach the beginner the basic techniques of quilting. Because miniquilts are completed so quickly – most of them within a few hours – it is possible to gain experience and confidence in a very short time. Most of these miniquilts have been planned to be just about foolproof!
Note All seam allowances are 6 mm, unless stated otherwise.

Rabbits (photograph on p. 12)

The contrasting navy, white and red colours give this quilt an old-world charm. Cheesecloth was used for the faces, arms and pinafores, and checks for the dresses. The hearts were painted. Complete this quilt in one morning and surprise your child.

Measurements
☐ Size of quilt, 41 cm x 41 cm
☐ Size of middle block, 37 cm x 37 cm
☐ Size of each block, 12 cm x 12 cm
☐ Number of blocks, 9

Materials
☐ Off-white cheesecloth/cotton for 10 patches of template A (ears), 5 patches of template D (head), 10 of template B (arms) and 5 of template C (pinafore), 15 cm
☐ Red fabric for 10 patches of templates E and F, 10 patches of templates G and H and the border strips, 25 cm
☐ Remnants of various checked fabrics for 5 patches of template I (upper body) and 5 patches of template J (dress)
☐ Off-white fabric for heart blocks and for backing, 25 cm
☐ Navy blue fabric for 5 patches of template L (heart), 10 cm
☐ Navy blue checked fabric for border and loops, 25 cm
☐ Thin batting, 45 cm x 45 cm

☐ Black and brown embroidery thread for face
☐ Red fabric paint (optional)

Assembling
☐ Make templates of the various parts, trace the outlines onto the different fabrics and cut them out.

Rabbit block (make 5)
The rabbits are made in 4 sections: the head, the arms, the lower body and the ears.
☐ Head: Stitch a red E and F onto both sides of an off-white D.
☐ Arms: Stitch an off-white B onto both sides of the red and navy checked I. Baste an off-white C that is slightly frayed onto the middle of check J. (The hearts are embroidered or painted beforehand.) Stitch the head onto the arms. Continue by stitching the lower body onto the arms (K on p. 13).
☐ Ears: Stitch 2 ears (template A) together, with right sides facing. Trim the seam allowance, turn the ears inside out and press. Place the ears at the top of the rabbit block with the raw edges together (make sure that the ears are placed in the middle of the head) and baste.

Heart block
☐ Measure the completed rabbit block. If all 4 sides are not exactly the same length, cut off excess fabric.
☐ Cut 4 off-white squares according to the measurements of the rabbit block.
☐ Place a navy heart (template L on p. 13) diagonally on top of an off-white square and machine appliqué.

Middle block
☐ Assemble 3 rows as follows:
Row 1: rabbit block + heart block + rabbit block
Row 2: heart block + rabbit block + heart block

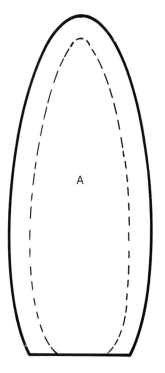

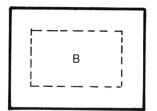

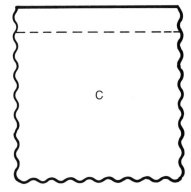

Row 3: rabbit block + heart block + rabbit block
☐ Stitch these 3 rows together.
☐ Press the completed middle block.

9

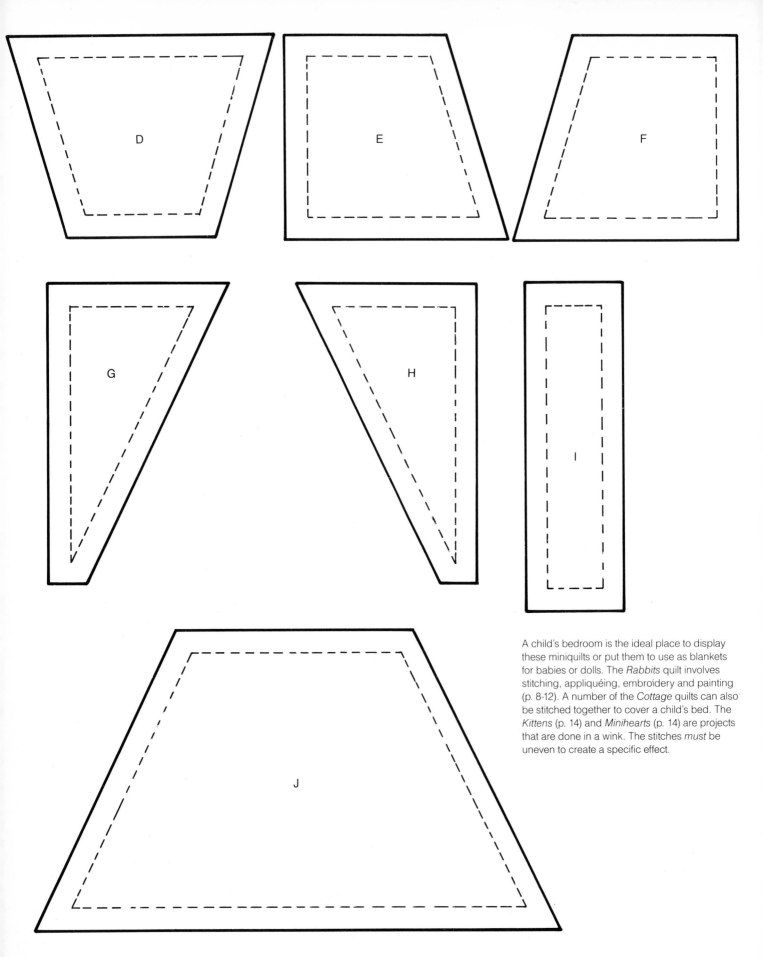

A child's bedroom is the ideal place to display these miniquilts or put them to use as blankets for babies or dolls. The *Rabbits* quilt involves stitching, appliquéing, embroidery and painting (p. 8-12). A number of the *Cottage* quilts can also be stitched together to cover a child's bed. The *Kittens* (p. 14) and *Minihearts* (p. 14) are projects that are done in a wink. The stitches *must* be uneven to create a specific effect.

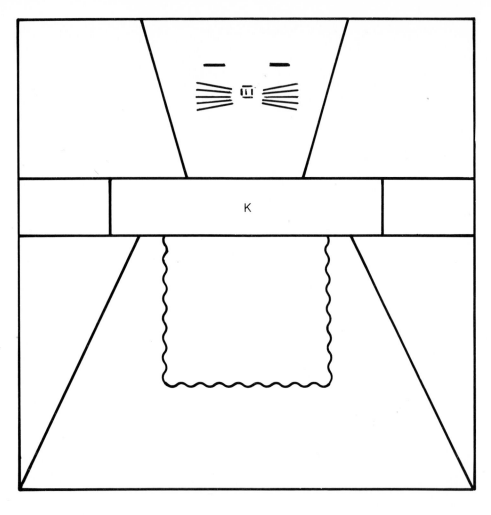

L

Borders
☐ Cut 2 navy checked fabric strips according to the length of the vertical sides (± 38 cm) and 3 cm wide and stitch onto both sides of middle block.
☐ Cut 2 navy checked fabric strips according to the length of the horizontal sides (± 42 cm) and 3 cm wide and stitch onto the top and bottom.
☐ Press the top.

Layers
☐ Cut a backing and the batting, each measuring 45 cm x 45 cm.
☐ Layer the backing, the batting and the top and baste (p. 6).

Quilting
☐ Quilt (p. 6-7) along the stitching lines and around the hearts.

Binding
☐ Trim the edges.
☐ Cut a red strip of 170 cm x 5 cm and bind the quilt (p. 7-8).

Finishing
For the eyes and nose, use 3 threads of black embroidery thread together. Make 2 horizontal stitches for the eyes in the top third of the head, and 3 vertical stitches close together for the nose. Use brown embroidery thread to make 4 lines of whiskers on each side of the nose.
Note The eyes, nose and whiskers are stitched only through the top layer, not through the entire quilt.
☐ Fix the apron and the ears to the top of the quilt with a few stitches to keep them down.
☐ Applying fabric paint to the apron: Draw a square of ± 5 cm x 5 cm on a piece of cardboard or plastic and draw a heart in the centre. Cut it out. Place the template with the heart-shaped opening in the middle of the apron and apply the red fabric paint with a small paintbrush.
☐ Loops: Cut 4 navy checked fabric strips of 10 cm x 5 cm. Fold them in half lengthwise with reverse sides together and press the fold. Fold each of the long raw edges 6 mm to the inside and top-stitch the 2 folded edges together. Neatly stitch the short ends to the top of the quilt.

Picnic time

If you wake up one morning feeling creative and you want to put something together on the spur of the moment, this quilt is the answer. The blocks are stitched together haphazardly, without any particular colour plan. You may add as many borders as you like, of whatever width. If you feel like taking more trouble, you could quilt along the borders, diagonally across the blocks, or do heart designs in the blocks. Instead of a picnic rug, this quilt could become a baby's blanket or a knee-rug for Granny!

Measurements
- Size of quilt, 110 cm x 110 cm
- Size of middle block, 100 cm x 100 cm
- Size of each block, 10 cm x 10 cm
- Number of blocks, 36
- Width of borders, 7 cm, 9 cm, 6 cm and 12 cm respectively

Materials
- 3 different red and blue checked fabrics for blocks and borders, ± 50 cm each
- Matching fabric for backing, 1 m
- Checked fabric for binding, 50 cm
- Thin batting, 120 cm x 120 cm

Assembling

Middle block
- Cut 36 different checked fabric squares of 10 cm x 10 cm, arrange in 6 rows of 6 squares each (6 x 6 = 36) and stitch together.
- Press the completed middle block of the quilt.

Borders
- Cut 2 checked fabric strips of ± 55 cm x 7 cm and stitch onto both sides of the middle block.
- Cut 2 checked fabric strips of ± 66 cm x 7 cm and stitch onto the top and bottom.
- Cut 2 strips in a different checked fabric of ± 66 cm x 9 cm and stitch onto both sides.
- Cut 2 strips of ± 80 cm x 9 cm and stitch onto the top and bottom.
- Repeat for third and fourth borders,

This *Picnic time* quilt is one of the easiest projects in the book. The dishcloth hanging out of the basket is simply made to a smaller scale and then treated with bleach to give it a "used" appearance.

of which the strips are 80/90 cm x 6 cm and 90/113 cm x 12 cm respectively. *Note* Feel free to add as many strips and to vary the width as you please. Follow your creative instincts.

Layers
- Cut a backing and the batting, each measuring 120 cm x 120 cm.
- Layer the backing, the batting and the top and baste (p. 6).

Quilting
- Quilt (p. 6-7) along the stitching lines to achieve a puffed effect.

Note Instead of quilting, use embroidery thread (or any other rough thread or yarn) to sew a single stitch right through the quilt at each corner of each block and knot the ends on the right side. The loose ends of the thread look like bows. This method is much quicker than quilting.

Binding
- Trim the edges.
- Cut a checked fabric strip of 4,5 m x 6 cm and bind the quilt (p. 7-8).

Kittens (photograph on p. 11)

If you have difficulty sewing even-sized stitches, this quilt allows you to sew your stitches as randomly as you like!

There are hundreds of possibilities for this technique – use it for clothing, cushions, towels, pot-holders or an unconventional wall-hanging.

Measurements
☐ Size, 12 cm x 12 cm

Materials
☐ Blue remnants for kittens and backing
☐ Coarse off-white fabric for background
☐ Pink and navy embroidery thread
☐ Thin batting

Assembling

Top
☐ Make a template of each of the kitten designs below.

☐ Trace the outline of each template onto the blue fabric.
Hint Iron Vilene to the back of the fabric. This makes it easier to handle and cut.
☐ Cut out the kittens.
☐ Cut 2 off-white squares of 12 cm x 12 cm.
☐ Paste a kitten, reverse side down, roughly in the centre of each off-white square.

Layers
☐ Cut 2 blue squares of 15 cm x 15 cm for the backing.
☐ Cut 2 batting squares of 12 cm x 12 cm.
☐ Layer the backing, the batting and the top and baste (p. 6).

"Binding"
☐ Fold the edge of the blue backing around to the top of the quilt and fold in a small hem to form a "binding" of about 1 cm.
☐ Baste the "binding" and stitch onto the off-white top with small invisible stitches.

Finishing
☐ Using 3 threads of navy embroidery thread, sew uneven stitches along the outer edges of the kittens through all 3 layers of fabric.
☐ Sew small basting stitches flush with the blue edge.
☐ Finish the quilts by sewing a bow at the neck of each kitten with 6 threads of pink embroidery thread.

Minihearts (photograph on p. 11)

This tiny heart quilt should go well with *Kittens* (opposite) in a nursery or child's room.

Measurements
☐ Size, 11 cm x 8 cm

Materials
☐ Blue remnants for hearts and backing
☐ Coarse off-white fabric for background
☐ Thin batting

Assembling

Top
☐ Make a template of the heart on p. 63.
☐ Trace the outline of the template twice onto the blue fabric.
☐ Cut out 2 hearts.
☐ Cut out an off-white rectangle of 11 cm x 8 cm for the background.
☐ Paste the hearts reverse side down on the off-white background.

Layers
☐ Cut batting of 11 cm x 8 cm.
☐ Cut a blue backing of 13 cm x 10 cm.
☐ Layer the backing, the batting and the top and baste (p. 6).

"Binding"
☐ See the instructions for *Kittens* (first column).

Finishing
☐ Using 6 embroidery threads together, make 2 pink bows and sew onto the top centre of each heart.

Stripes (photograph on p. 33)

Our striped quilt is probably the easiest project in this book. All that is needed is to stitch together 3 cm strips (or any other width), add borders, do a bit of quilting (if you wish) bind the quilt.

Measurements
☐ Size of quilt, 54 cm x 40 cm
☐ Size of middle block, 39 cm x 25 cm
☐ Length of each strip, 40 cm

- ☐ Width of each strip, 3 cm
- ☐ Number of strips, 13

Materials
- ☐ Blue remnants for strips, 50 cm
- ☐ Red fabric for inner border and binding, 20 cm
- ☐ Blue fabric for outer border, 10 cm
- ☐ Matching fabric for backing, 45 cm
- ☐ Thin batting, 45 cm x 45 cm

Assembling

Middle block
- ☐ Cut 13 blue strips of 40 cm x 3 cm each.
- ☐ Stitch the strips together at random along the long edges – some even reverse side up!
- ☐ Trim the top and bottom edges to give the middle block a length of 39 cm.

Borders
- ☐ Cut 2 red strips of 39 cm x 3 cm and stitch onto both sides of the middle block.
- ☐ Cut 2 red strips of 29 cm x 3 cm and stitch onto the top and the bottom.
- ☐ Cut 2 blue strips of 42,5 cm x 6,5 cm and stitch onto both sides.
- ☐ Cut 2 blue strips of 40 cm x 6,5 cm and stitch onto the top and the bottom.

Layers
- ☐ Cut a backing and the batting, each measuring 58 cm x 45 cm.
- ☐ Layer the backing, the batting and the top and baste (p. 6).

Quilting
- ☐ The quilt in the photograph (p. 33) has not been quilted, but if you wish, you can quilt (p. 6-7) along the stitching lines.

Binding
- ☐ Trim the edges.
- ☐ Cut a red strip of 2 m x 4 cm and bind the quilt (p. 7-8).

Yo-yo (photograph on p. 16)

For a brand-new quilting experience, create an old-world quilt in dark colours. The yo-yo quilt is completely handmade and it is an ideal task to pass the time in the dentist's waiting room or whenever you have a spare moment. As a wall-hanging this quilt will immediately catch the eye. It also makes a very special doll's blanket. By cutting larger circles you can make a larger quilt.

Measurements
- ☐ Size, 13 cm x 13 cm

Materials
- ☐ Plain dark-coloured remnants

Assembling
- ☐ Make a template of the circle, trace the outline onto the remnants and cut out 64 circles.

- ☐ You can save a lot of time by stacking the remnants and cutting several circles at a time. Pin all the layers together and cut.
- ☐ Use a double thread with a knot at the end.
- ☐ Fold the edges of the circles in ± 5 mm.
- ☐ Sew basting stitches along the fold and pull the thread tight to draw the circle to the inside.
- ☐ Fasten the pleats in the middle, cut the thread and flatten the circles.
- ☐ Arrange the circles in 8 rows of 8 circles each.
- ☐ Sew the circles together with a few stitches where they meet.
- ☐ Press the quilt on both sides.

Trellis (photograph on p. 16)

About two hundred years ago a group of settlers arrived in Pennsylvania in America and founded a unique community. They were the followers of Jacob Amman and in time became known as the Amish. The members of this religious movement believe that they should adhere strictly to biblical instructions and that they should make a living from the soil.

The simple Amish way of life has been preserved through the years, and is reflected dramatically in their handmade quilts. The beautiful quilts are made of plain dark and especially black fabrics. (Prints are regarded as frivolous and extravagant.) Black is the basic colour of all their clothing.

The geometric designs of the Amish quilts are centuries old and today the severe lines are still very striking – in a modern as well as in a traditional setting. The trellis is one of the typical Amish designs. Only two plain fabrics are used to represent the trellises of the traditional wooden fences on the Amish farms.

Measurements
- ☐ Size, 30 cm x 28 cm

Materials
- ☐ Black fabric for outer border and trelliswork, 20 cm
- ☐ Purple fabric for inner border and trelliswork, 20 cm
- ☐ Dark pink (or any other plain fabric) for backing, 25 cm
- ☐ Thin batting, 34 cm x 32 cm

Assembling

Middle block
- ☐ Cut 3 black strips and 2 purple strips of 18 cm x 4,5 cm.
- ☐ Arrange the purple strips between the black strips and stitch the long edges together.
- ☐ Press the seams in the direction of the black strips.

Borders
- ☐ Cut 2 purple strips according to the length of the vertical sides (purple strips included) and 4,5 cm wide and

A few examples of the effectively simple and austere quilts of the Amish folk. These deeply religious people, who live in communities throughout the world but particularly in the United States, do not believe in decorating themselves or their homes lavishly. Notice that the faces of the dolls are featureless. The reason for this is the Amish interpretation of Deuteronomy 5:8 wherein God's people are forbidden to make images of themselves. Above are three *Trellis* quilts (p. 15-16), in the centre are the *Yo-yo* quilt (p. 15) which consists simply of circles of fabric gathered and stitched together, and the *Amish mini* (p. 17). Below is a greater variety of the same quilts in different colours.

stitch onto both sides of middle block.

☐ Cut 2 purple strips according to the length of horizontal sides and 4,5 cm wide and stitch onto top and bottom.
☐ Cut 2 black strips according to the new length of horizontal sides and 4,5 cm wide and stitch onto top and bottom.
☐ Cut 2 black strips according to the new length of the vertical sides (black strips included) and 4,5 cm wide and stitch onto both sides.
☐ Press the top.

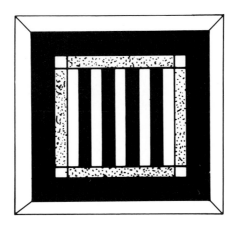

Layers
The layers of this quilt are put together by a simple method which differs from that recommended for most of the other quilts in this book.
☐ Cut the backing and the batting exactly the same size as the top.
☐ Place the backing over the batting, reverse side down, and then the top right side down on the backing. Baste.
☐ Start in the middle of one of the sides and stitch right round through all three layers, leaving an opening of 10 cm.
☐ Trim the raw edges and cut away diagonally at the corners.
☐ Turn the quilt inside out, press thoroughly and close the opening with invisible stitches.

Quilting
☐ Normally no quilting is done on the *Trellis*, but if you wish, quilt along the stitching lines, or quilt (p. 6-7) a design on the trelliswork.

Amish mini (photograph on p. 16)

It is a pleasure to make this very simple and typical Amish quilt. The strong contrasting colours make it a striking wall-hanging.

Measurements
☐ Size of quilt, 18 cm x 18 cm
☐ Size of middle block, 7 cm x 7 cm
☐ Width of borders, 0,5 cm, 1 cm and 3,5 cm respectively

Materials
☐ Sea-green, red and purple remnants
☐ Purple fabric for backing, 22 cm
☐ Thin batting, 20 cm x 20 cm

Assembling

Middle block
☐ Cut 5 sea-green and 4 purple strips of 8 cm x 1,5 cm.
☐ Stitch the strips together (see diagram below).
☐ Trim the stitched sets to form a square of 7 cm x 7 cm.
☐ Press the middle block.

Borders
☐ Cut 4 red strips of 7 cm x 1,5 cm.
☐ Stitch 2 of the red strips onto the top and bottom of the middle block.
☐ Cut 4 sea-green blocks of 1,5 cm x 1,5 cm and stitch onto both ends of the 2 remaining red strips.
☐ Stitch these 2 strips onto the vertical sides of the middle block.
☐ Cut 4 purple strips of 8 cm x 3 cm.

☐ Stitch a purple strip onto each vertical side of the middle block.
☐ Cut 4 sea-green blocks of 3 cm x 3 cm and stitch onto both ends of the 2 remaining purple strips.
☐ Stitch these strips onto the top and bottom of the middle block.
☐ Cut a black strip of 68 cm x 5 cm and cut off 2 sets of 11 cm each. Stitch the black sets onto the top and bottom.
☐ Cut the rest of the black strip into 2 sets of 18 cm each and stitch onto the sides.
☐ Press the completed top thoroughly.

Layers
☐ Cut a purple backing of 22 cm x 22 cm and batting of 20 cm x 20 cm.
☐ Layer the backing, the batting and the top and baste (p. 6).

Quilting
☐ Quilt (p. 6-7) along all the stitching lines.

"Binding"
☐ Fold the purple backing forward and fold the edges in 6 mm to form a hem.
☐ Stitch the hem onto the black border using invisible stitches.

Flourbags (photograph on p. 18)

If Grandma had known what good sewing material flourbags are, she would have saved each one carefully and bequeathed it to her favourite granddaughter! In those days flourbags were bleached to remove the print and then used as snow-white dishcloths. The bags are made of 100% cotton and are therefore ideal for candlewicking. The unbleached bags can also be turned into many interesting quilted articles, for example a pot-holder (see photograph), a bread blanket, a cloth for keeping scones hot or simply as a decoration on the kitchen wall or kitchen table. The old-fashioned wording and printed logo make it unique – do you still remember pounds and ounces? Use a 25 lb bag for this quilt and a 5 lb bag for the pot-holder.

Measurements
☐ Size, 58 cm x 50 cm

Now you know what to do with Grandma's old flourbags, whether bleached or not — they can come into their own as heirlooms turned to good use as pot-holders or bread blankets (p. 17-18). You might like to do quilting around the logo and the printing. The large flourbag boasts the date of 1939!

Materials
☐ A 25 lb flourbag for the front
☐ A flourbag or other off-white fabric for backing and binding, 65 cm
☐ Thin batting, 62 cm x 54 cm

Assembling

Middle block
☐ Draw the string at the seam of the bag or cut it open (if you have difficulty) and iron flat.

Layers
☐ Cut a backing and the batting, each measuring 62 cm x 54 cm (slightly larger than the top).
☐ Layer the backing, the batting and the top and baste (p. 6).

Quilting
☐ Trace the desired quilting pattern onto the top and quilt (p. 6-7) along these lines as well as around the words and logo.
☐ Instead of quilting you may do candlewick embroidery on the quilt.

Binding
☐ Trim the edges.
☐ Cut a strip of 2,4 m x 5 cm and bind the quilt (p. 7-8).

Rainbow (photograph on p. 19)

The tumbling colours of this quilt represent a rainbow. A single template is used to cut red, yellow, green, purple and plenty of white or off-white patches. The darker, heavier colours are arranged along the lower part of the wall-hanging.

Measurements
☐ Size of quilt, 100 cm x 42 cm
☐ Size of each block, 8 cm x 5 cm
☐ Number of blocks, 170

Materials
☐ White or off-white fabric for backing, 1,5 m
☐ Green, yellow, pink, blue, navy, purple, dark pink, light brown (or shades of all these colours), white, and off-white remnants for a total of 170 patches of template A
☐ Thin batting, 75 cm
☐ Embroidery thread of various colours for quilting on coloured patches

Assembling

Top
☐ Use the template (above right) to trace the outline onto the different fabrics and cut out 170 blocks.
Note The rotary cutter will do this job in a jiffy (see p. 4-5).
☐ Arrange the blocks at random in 12 rows (see photograph on facing page).
Note The darker colours are arranged along the borders, and the first few rows increase by a single block.
☐ Stitch the 12 vertical rows together.
☐ Press the top.

Layers
☐ Layer the backing, the batting and the top and baste (p. 6).
☐ Trim the backing and the batting to match the stepped top.

Quilting
☐ Draw horizontal lines, 6 mm apart,

18

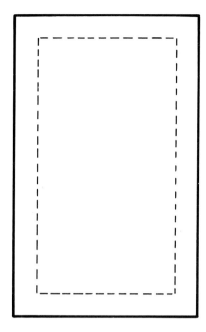

on all the off-white blocks and vertical lines on the coloured blocks.

☐ Quilt (p. 6-7) along these lines up to ± 6 mm from the edges, as well as along all the stitching lines.

Finishing

☐ Fold a 6 mm seam toward the inside, and slip-stitch the folded edges together.

☐ Sew 6 curtain rings at the back of the wall-hanging along the top edge so as to be invisible from the front. Push a thin rod through the rings.

The interesting shape and colour scheme make this *Rainbow* quilt (p. 18) something quite special. Light-coloured patches are stitched together in rows of different lengths with all the darker colours along the lower edge. The occasional bright patches of colour represent the front part of the rainbow which is disappearing.

Single Irish chain (photograph on p. 21)

The quick-cut, quick-stitch method works very well for the Irish chains. Three different chains are described: the single, the double and the triple chains. Although they do not look similar, the method is basically the same. The quilts can be made bigger or smaller by simply cutting wider or narrower strips.

Measurements
☐ Size of quilt, 65 cm x 52 cm
☐ Size of middle block, 46 cm x 33 cm
☐ Size of each block, 6,5 cm x 6,5 cm
☐ Width of borders, 2,5 cm and 5,5 cm respectively

Materials
☐ Pink fabric, 50 cm
☐ White fabric, 1 m
☐ Matching fabric for backing, 60 cm
☐ Thin batting, 70 cm x 58 cm

Assembling

Middle block
☐ Cut 4 pink strips of 115 cm x 4 cm and 2 white strips of 115 cm x 4 cm.
☐ Stitch 3 strips together in the sequence: pink, white, pink.

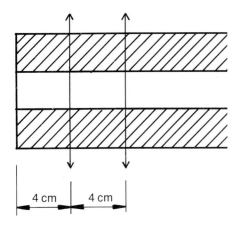

Note Stitch the strips from left to right and the next seam from right to left. This will keep your work square.
☐ Make a second set of strips.
☐ Press the seams in the direction of the pink fabric.

☐ Cut each of these strip sets into 36 sets of 4 cm wide.
☐ Cut 1 pink strip of 115 cm x 4 cm and 2 white strips of 115 cm x 4 cm.
☐ Stitch the three strips together in the sequence: white, pink, white.

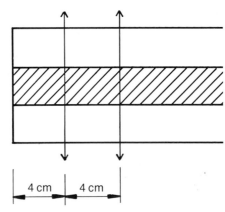

☐ Press the seams in the direction of the pink fabric.
☐ Cut this strip set into 18 sets of 4 cm wide.
☐ Stitch the 2 pink-white-pink sets and the 1 white-pink-white set together.

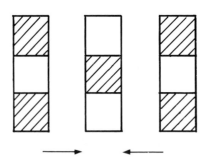

☐ Make 18 of these units, each consisting of 9 squares.
☐ Cut 17 white squares of 9 cm x 9 cm.
☐ Stitch the pink-white squares and the white squares together in 7 rows of 4 squares each. Stitch these 7 rows together (see above right).

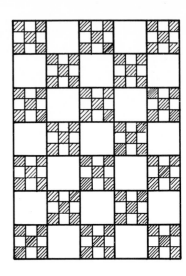

Borders
☐ Cut 2 pink strips of 60 cm x 4 cm and stitch onto both sides of the middle block.
☐ Cut 2 pink strips of 40 cm x 4 cm and stitch onto the top and bottom.
☐ Cut 2 white strips of 76 cm x 6,5 cm and stitch onto both sides.
☐ Cut 2 white strips of 45 cm x 6,5 cm and stitch onto the top and bottom.
☐ Trace the heart on p. 63 (*Friendship*) onto the white border. Onto the white blocks, trace the heart design given below.

Layers
☐ Cut a backing and the batting, each measuring 70 cm x 58 cm.
☐ Layer the backing, the batting and the top and baste (p. 6).

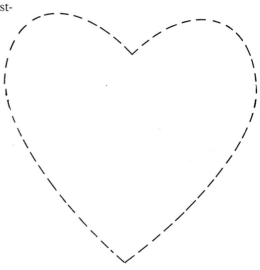

Quilting

☐ Quilt (p. 6-7) on the lines of the hearts and then diagonally across all the pink blocks. In addition, quilt little hearts along the outside white border.

Binding

☐ Trim the edges.
☐ Cut a pink strip of 2,4 m x 5 cm and bind the quilt (p. 7-8).

The *Single Irish chain* quilt, above (p. 20), is a good choice for a first project. It is very easy to keep track of the two colours. The *Five-block quilt*, below (p. 29), is child's play and the floral border looks most attractive.

Double Irish chain (photograph on facing page)

Measurements
☐ Size of quilt, 58 cm x 40 cm
☐ Size of middle block, 43 cm x 25 cm
☐ Width of borders, 2 cm, 2 cm and 3,5 cm respectively

Materials
☐ Dark green fabric for blocks and outer border, 25 cm
☐ Red/green fabric for blocks, inner border and binding, 50 cm
☐ Off-white fabric for blocks and backing, 75 cm
☐ Red fabric for inner border, 20 cm
☐ Thin batting, 60 cm x 44 cm

Assembling

Block 1 of middle block

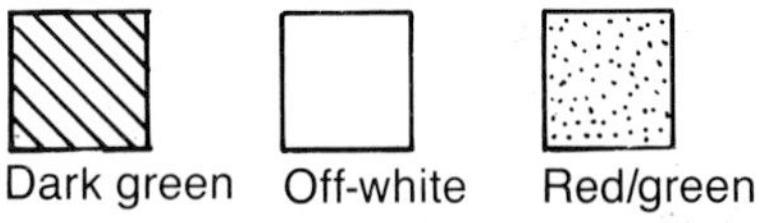

Dark green Off-white Red/green

☐ Cut 9 dark green strips of 50 cm x 3 cm, 9 red/green strips of 50 cm x 3 cm and 3 off-white strips of 50 cm x 3 cm.
☐ Stitch these strips together in 3 different combinations: units A, B, C.
☐ Unit A: Stitch together 5 strips in the colour combination: red/green, dark green, off-white, dark green, red/green.

Unit A

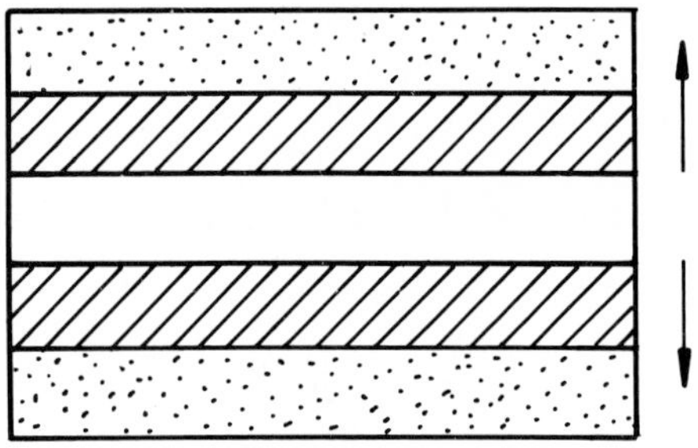

Hint Stitch every next seam in the opposite direction; in other words, the first seam from left to right, but instead of starting at the top with the next seam, stitch from the bottom up. This will keep your strip set square.

☐ Press the seams in the direction of the arrows.
☐ Stitch together the strips of units B and C as follows:

Unit B

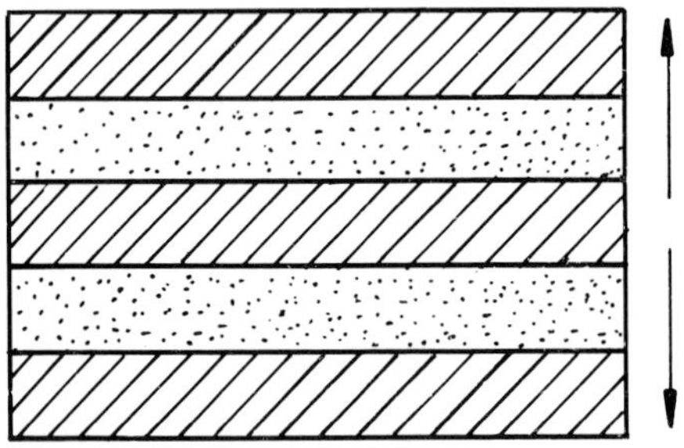

Unit C

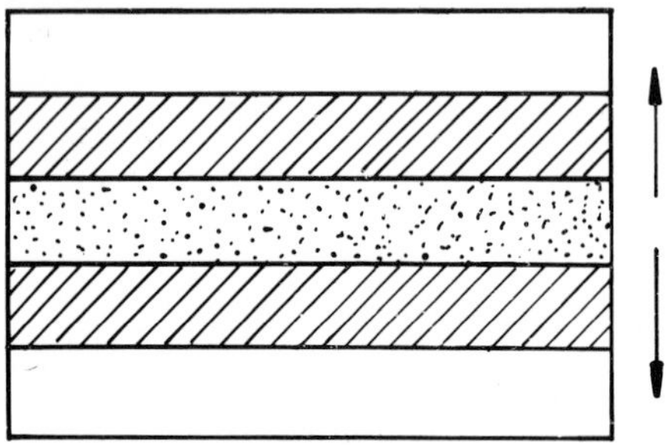

☐ Press the seams in the direction of the arrows.
☐ Cut units A, B and C into sets in the width as follows:

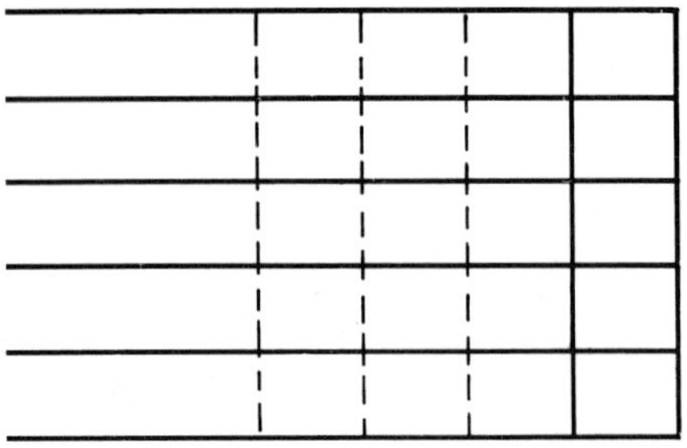

Unit A: 16 sets of 3 cm each and label them A
Unit B: 16 sets of 3 cm each and label them B
Unit C: 8 sets of 3 cm each and label them C
☐ Arrange and stitch the different sets of units A-C together as shown above:

Block 1

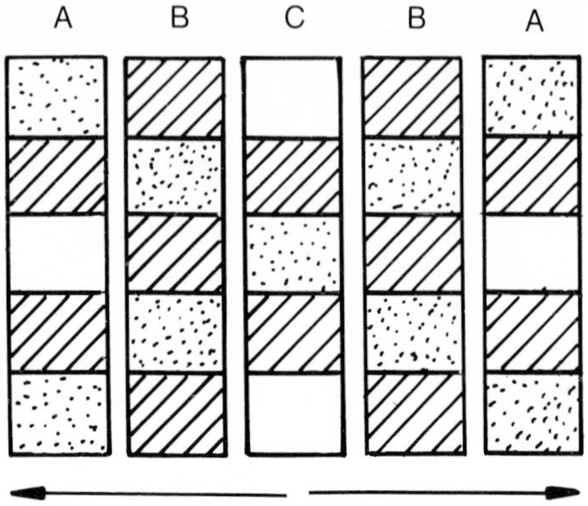

☐ Press the seams in the direction of the arrows. You should begin to form some idea of what the end result will look like.

Block 2 of middle block
☐ *Unit D:* Cut 1 off-white strip of 50 cm x 7,2 cm and to each side of it stitch a dark green strip of 50 cm x 3 cm (cut beforehand).

Unit D

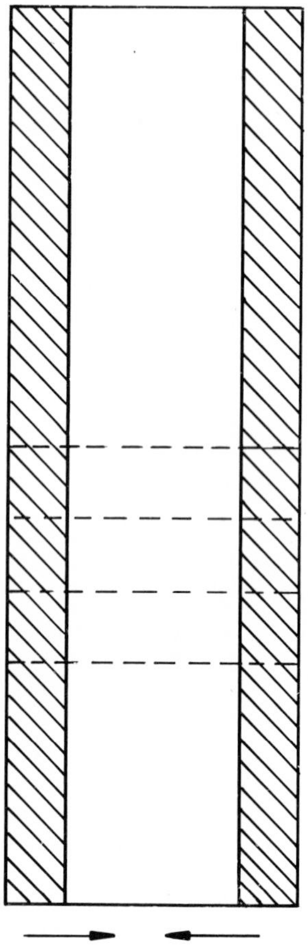

☐ Press the seams in the direction of the arrows.
☐ Cut unit D into 14 sets of 3 cm each.

After you have made these quilts, Christmas will never be the same! The tree decorations are made without any difficulty according to the shadow-appliqué method (see *Christmas decorations*, p. 64-66). On the wall is the *Bouquet* quilt with its red embroidery (p. 62-63) — a most suitable gift for a special person. Above the *Bouquet* quilt is a small *Log cabin* (p. 32-33). To the left is the *Double Irish chain* quilt (instructions facing) in red and green to set a festive Christmassy mood. With all its colours the *Flower garden* quilt, left (p. 44-45), takes a little concentration, but once you've got the hang of the technique a whole new world is opened to you.

☐ *Unit E:* Cut 7 off-white strips of
11 cm x 7 cm.
☐ Stitch together the sets of units D
and E

Block 2

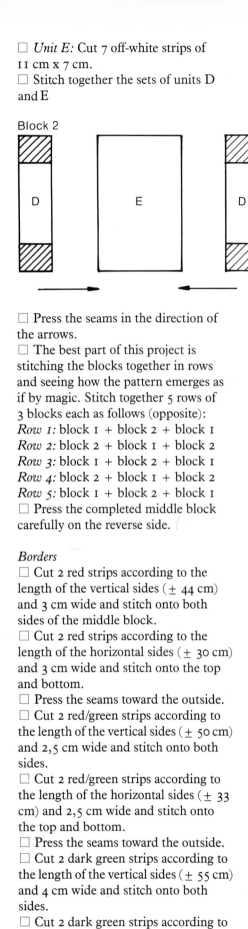

☐ Press the seams in the direction of
the arrows.
☐ The best part of this project is
stitching the blocks together in rows
and seeing how the pattern emerges as
if by magic. Stitch together 5 rows of
3 blocks each as follows (opposite):
Row 1: block 1 + block 2 + block 1
Row 2: block 2 + block 1 + block 2
Row 3: block 1 + block 2 + block 1
Row 4: block 2 + block 1 + block 2
Row 5: block 1 + block 2 + block 1
☐ Press the completed middle block
carefully on the reverse side.

Borders
☐ Cut 2 red strips according to the
length of the vertical sides (± 44 cm)
and 3 cm wide and stitch onto both
sides of the middle block.
☐ Cut 2 red strips according to the
length of the horizontal sides (± 30 cm)
and 3 cm wide and stitch onto the top
and bottom.
☐ Press the seams toward the outside.
☐ Cut 2 red/green strips according to
the length of the vertical sides (± 50 cm)
and 2,5 cm wide and stitch onto both
sides.
☐ Cut 2 red/green strips according to
the length of the horizontal sides (± 33
cm) and 2,5 cm wide and stitch onto
the top and bottom.
☐ Press the seams toward the outside.
☐ Cut 2 dark green strips according to
the length of the vertical sides (± 55 cm)
and 4 cm wide and stitch onto both
sides.
☐ Cut 2 dark green strips according to
the length of the horizontal sides (± 40

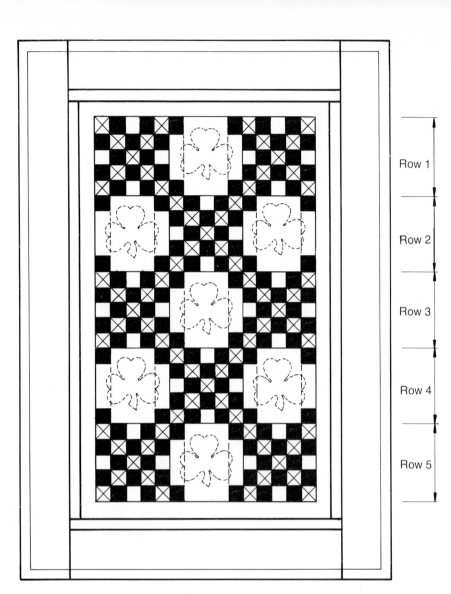

24

cm) and 4 cm wide and stitch onto the top and bottom.

Layers
☐ Cut an off-white backing and the batting, each measuring 62 cm x 44 cm.
☐ Layer the backing, the batting and the top and baste (p. 6).

Quilting
☐ Make a template of the leaf (below left) and trace the outline onto the off-white blocks.
☐ Quilt (p. 6-7) along the lines of the leaves and around the 7 large off-white blocks.

Binding
☐ Trim the sides.
☐ Cut a red/green strip of 2,1 m x 4 cm and bind the quilt (p. 7-8).

Triple Irish chain (photograph on p. 28)

This variation of the Irish chains is just as easy as the other two. Only a few steps are added.

Measurements
☐ Size of quilt, 76 cm x 76 cm
☐ Size of middle block, 62 cm x 62 cm
☐ Width of borders, 2,5 cm, 2 cm and 2 cm respectively

Materials
☐ Navy blue print (1), 50 cm
☐ Navy blue fabric (2), 60 cm
☐ Light blue fabric (3), 50 cm
☐ White fabric (4), 25 cm
☐ Matching fabric for backing, 1,25 m
☐ Thin batting, 80 cm x 80 cm

Assembling

Middle block
Hint Fold all fabric in half with selvages together.

☐ Cut 5 strips of navy blue print of 106 cm x 3 cm, 9 navy blue strips of 106 cm x 3 cm, 6 light blue strips of 106 cm x 3 cm, 2 white strips of 106 cm x 3 cm and 12 white squares of 9 cm x 9 cm.

☐ Make the 5 strip sets by stitching strips together according to the colour codes. To keep the work square, follow the instructions on p. 6.
Note One of the strip sets consists of only 3 strips, and all the others consist of 5 strips (see below).

Strip set 1

2
3
4
3
2

Strip set 2

3
4
3

Strip set 3

2
1
2
1
2

Strip set 4

1
2
3
2
1

Strip set 5

3
2
1
2
3

1 Navy blue print
2 Navy blue
3 Light blue
4 White

□ Press the seams of the completed sets in the direction of the arrows.

□ Cut the 3 cm strip sets as follows:

Strip set 1: 24 sets
Strip set 2: 24 sets
Strip set 3: 26 sets
Strip set 4: 26 sets
Strip set 5: 13 sets

□ Combine 13 checked blocks out of 2 sets of strip sets 3 and 4 each and 1 set of strip set 5 (see below). Stitch together.

□ Press the seams in the direction of the arrows.

□ Stitch a set of strip set 2 onto the top and bottom of each of the 12 white squares.

□ Press the seams in the direction of the arrows.

□ Stitch a set of strip set 1 onto both sides of each white square.

26

☐ Press the seams toward the inside.
☐ Combine the checked fabric blocks and lighter blocks as shown below. Row 1 will consist of: checked fabric block, lighter block, checked fabric block, lighter block, checked fabric block.
☐ Arrange the blocks for the middle block in 5 rows of 5 blocks each (see below).

Row 1: check + light + check + light + check

Row 2: light + check + light + check + light

Row 3: check + light + check + light + check

Row 4: light + check + light + check + light

Row 5: check + light + check + light + check

☐ Stitch the rows together and take care to match the seams and corners exactly where they meet.
☐ Press the completed middle block.

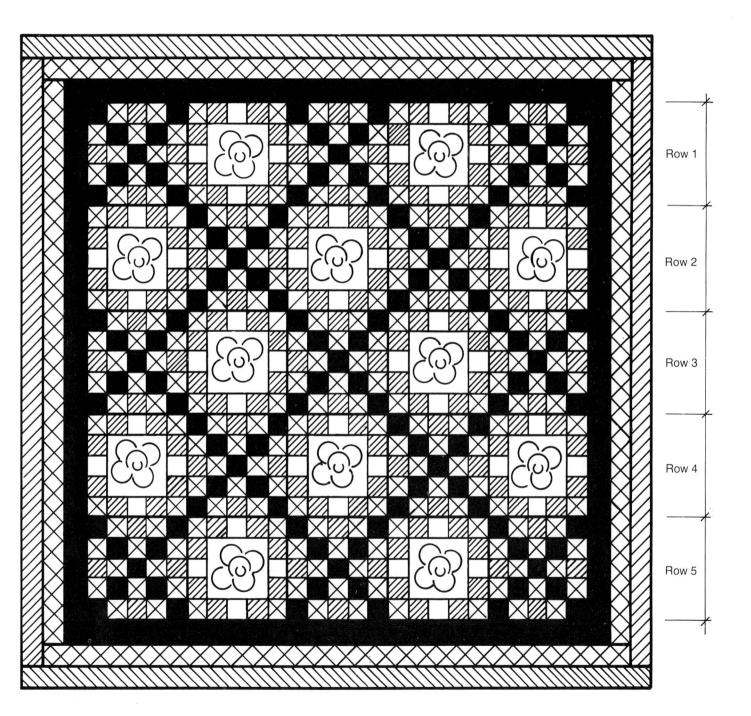

Row 1

Row 2

Row 3

Row 4

Row 5

Borders

☐ As the lengths of the sides may differ from the following measurements, it is important to measure the sides and to cut your strips accordingly (p. 8).
☐ Cut 2 navy blue print strips of 70 cm x 4 cm and stitch onto both sides (the longest sides) of the middle block.
☐ Cut 2 navy print strips of 65 cm x 4 cm and stitch onto the top and bottom.
☐ Cut 2 navy blue strips of 75,5 cm x 4 cm and stitch onto both sides.
☐ Cut 2 navy blue strips of 70 cm x 4 cm and stitch onto the top and bottom.
☐ Cut 2 light blue strips of 81 cm x 4 cm and stitch onto both sides.
☐ Cut 2 light blue strips of 75,5 cm x 4 cm and stitch onto the top and bottom.
☐ Carefully press the top.

Layers

☐ Cut a backing and the batting, each measuring 100 cm x 100 cm.
☐ Layer the backing, the batting and the top and baste (p. 6).

Quilting

☐ Trace the quilting design onto the 12 white blocks and quilt (p. 6-7).

☐ Quilt diagonally across all the navy blue blocks and along all the stitching lines of the borders.

Binding

☐ Trim the edges.
☐ Cut a strip of navy blue print of 3,5 m x 5 cm and bind the quilt (p. 7-8).

The *Triple Irish chain* quilt, above (p. 25-27), can be very striking if the colours of the fabrics are strongly contrasting. In the centre is *Nine hearts* (p. 46-47) with the hearts appliquéd by hand. Notice the interesting effect created by the echo quilting around the hearts. Below is the *Charms* quilt (p. 46) with the charms being 25 hearts each of a different colour and finished in blanket stitch with black embroidery thread.

Four-block quilt (photograph on p. 42)

This cute little quilt has so many possibilities and is so attractive that one feels inspired to make several of them.
A few remnants are all you need, and once you start stitching you will not be able to stop until you see the end result.

Measurements
☐ Size of quilt, 25 cm x 22,5 cm
☐ Size of middle block, 20,5 cm x 19 cm
☐ Width of borders, 0,5 cm and 1 cm respectively

Materials
☐ Light (pink and light brown), medium (light blue) and dark (navy blue) remnants
☐ Purple fabric for strips and backing (which will be folded forward to form the dark border), 32 cm
☐ Thin batting, 28 cm x 28 cm
☐ Purple ribbon of 1 cm wide, 50 cm (optional)

Assembling

Middle block
☐ Cut 28 squares of 4 cm x 4 cm in different colours (use a rotary cutter).
☐ Cut 4 light brown strips of 20 cm x 2,5 cm, 2 navy blue strips of 20 cm x 2,5 cm and 2 purple strips of 20 cm x 2,5 cm.
☐ Join a dark (navy or purple) strip to a light (light brown) strip.

☐ Make another 3 sets of light-dark strips.
☐ Press the seams in the direction of the dark strip.
☐ Cut the long strips along the width into light-dark sets of 2,5 cm wide.

☐ Stitch the light-dark sets together in pairs. Remember to turn reverse of the sets so that the dark and light squares end up in opposite corners.

☐ Make a total of 28 light-dark blocks.
☐ Arrange the blocks in 8 rows of 7 blocks each (only 3 horizontal rows are shown in the diagram) by alternating the light-dark squares with plain ones and stitch together.

☐ Carefully press the middle block.

Border
☐ Cut 2 light brown strips according to the length of the vertical sides (± 20 cm) and 2 cm wide and stitch onto both sides of the middle block.
☐ Cut 2 light brown strips according to the length of the horizontal sides (± 19 cm) and 2 cm wide and stitch onto the top and bottom.
☐ Cut 2 pink strips of 22 cm x 2,5 cm and stitch onto both sides.
☐ Cut 2 pink strips of 19,5 cm x 2,5 cm and stitch onto the top and bottom.

Layers
☐ Cut a backing of 32 cm x 32 cm and batting of 28 cm x 28 cm.
☐ Layer the backing, the batting and the top and baste (p. 6).

Quilting
☐ Quilt (p. 6-7) diagonally across the 4 cm squares and along the stitching lines of the borders.

"Binding"
☐ Trim the batting to match the edges of the top.
☐ Fold the backing forward and fold the edge in 6 mm.
☐ Sew the hem to the top with invisible stitches.

Finishing (optional)
☐ Sew the purple ribbon onto the top corners of the quilt and use them to tie the quilt to arm-rests, doors, bedheads, etc.

Five-block quilt (photograph on p. 21)

Only two colours, a light (white) and a dark (pink) fabric, are cut, sewn and finished with a floral fabric to produce this quilt. It can easily be enlarged to fit on a single bed – simply multiply the measurements by 4.

Measurements
☐ Size of quilt, 98 cm x 75 cm
☐ Size of each block, 12 cm x 12 cm
☐ Number of blocks, 35
☐ Width of borders, 2 cm, 4,5 cm and 3 cm respectively

Materials
☐ White fabric for blocks and backing, 1,5 m
☐ Pink fabric for blocks, 1,25 m
☐ Floral fabric for inner border, 25 cm

Assembling

Middle block
☐ Cut 4 pink strips of 115 cm x 4 cm and 2 white strips of 115 cm x 2 cm.
☐ Stitch a pink strip onto both sides of a white strip (as shown at top of p. 30).

☐ Make another strip set.
☐ Cut these strips along the width into 36 sets of 4 cm.

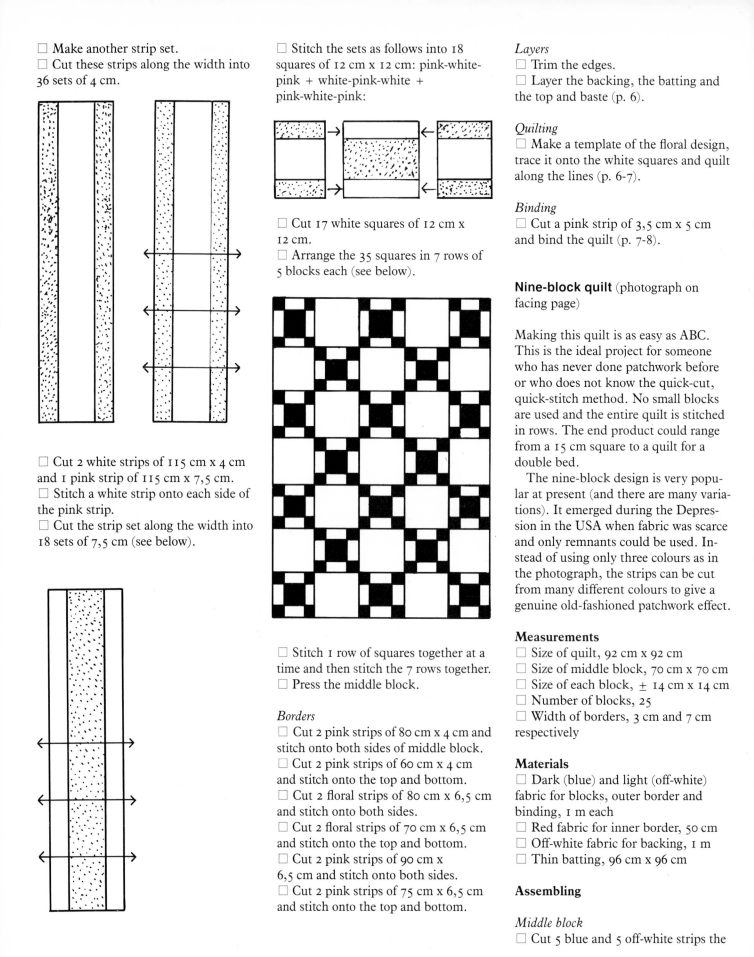

☐ Cut 2 white strips of 115 cm x 4 cm and 1 pink strip of 115 cm x 7,5 cm.
☐ Stitch a white strip onto each side of the pink strip.
☐ Cut the strip set along the width into 18 sets of 7,5 cm (see below).

☐ Stitch the sets as follows into 18 squares of 12 cm x 12 cm: pink-white-pink + white-pink-white + pink-white-pink:

☐ Cut 17 white squares of 12 cm x 12 cm.
☐ Arrange the 35 squares in 7 rows of 5 blocks each (see below).

☐ Stitch 1 row of squares together at a time and then stitch the 7 rows together.
☐ Press the middle block.

Borders
☐ Cut 2 pink strips of 80 cm x 4 cm and stitch onto both sides of middle block.
☐ Cut 2 pink strips of 60 cm x 4 cm and stitch onto the top and bottom.
☐ Cut 2 floral strips of 80 cm x 6,5 cm and stitch onto both sides.
☐ Cut 2 floral strips of 70 cm x 6,5 cm and stitch onto the top and bottom.
☐ Cut 2 pink strips of 90 cm x 6,5 cm and stitch onto both sides.
☐ Cut 2 pink strips of 75 cm x 6,5 cm and stitch onto the top and bottom.

Layers
☐ Trim the edges.
☐ Layer the backing, the batting and the top and baste (p. 6).

Quilting
☐ Make a template of the floral design, trace it onto the white squares and quilt along the lines (p. 6-7).

Binding
☐ Cut a pink strip of 3,5 cm x 5 cm and bind the quilt (p. 7-8).

Nine-block quilt (photograph on facing page)

Making this quilt is as easy as ABC. This is the ideal project for someone who has never done patchwork before or who does not know the quick-cut, quick-stitch method. No small blocks are used and the entire quilt is stitched in rows. The end product could range from a 15 cm square to a quilt for a double bed.

The nine-block design is very popular at present (and there are many variations). It emerged during the Depression in the USA when fabric was scarce and only remnants could be used. Instead of using only three colours as in the photograph, the strips can be cut from many different colours to give a genuine old-fashioned patchwork effect.

Measurements
☐ Size of quilt, 92 cm x 92 cm
☐ Size of middle block, 70 cm x 70 cm
☐ Size of each block, ± 14 cm x 14 cm
☐ Number of blocks, 25
☐ Width of borders, 3 cm and 7 cm respectively

Materials
☐ Dark (blue) and light (off-white) fabric for blocks, outer border and binding, 1 m each
☐ Red fabric for inner border, 50 cm
☐ Off-white fabric for backing, 1 m
☐ Thin batting, 96 cm x 96 cm

Assembling

Middle block
☐ Cut 5 blue and 5 off-white strips the

full width of the fabric and 6,5 cm wide.

Note If you find that you do not have enough strips, cut more.

☐ Stitch the strips together along the long edges in groups of 3:

Group A: blue + off-white + blue

Group B: off-white + blue + off-white

☐ Press the seams in the direction of the dark colour.

☐ Cut group A along the width into 26 sets of 6,5 cm wide, and group B into 13 sets of 6,5 cm wide.

☐ Stitch 3 sets together to form the basic nine-block design.

☐ Make 12 more similar blocks.

☐ Press the seams of the middle set (off-white + blue + off-white) alternately towards the left and the right sides.

☐ Measure a completed block – it will be about 16 cm x 16 cm.

☐ Cut 12 off-white blocks of 16 cm x 16 cm.

☐ Arrange the blocks in 5 rows of 5 blocks each (opposite). Stitch each row of 5 blocks together and then stitch the 5 rows together.

☐ Press the middle block carefully on the reverse side.

The *Nine-block* quilt (p. 30-32) in front of the chair is one of those projects that, having completed the first, you can't wait to try another in different shades or with smaller or larger blocks. Ideal for the beginner! The *Lightning* quilt (p. 41-44) in the background presents a challenge to someone who wants to experiment with a lot of colours.

Borders

☐ Cut 2 red strips according to the length of the vertical sides (± 70 cm) and 5 cm wide and stitch onto both sides of the completed middle block.

☐ Cut 2 red strips according to the length of the horizontal sides (± 78 cm) and 5 cm wide and stitch onto the top and bottom.

☐ Cut 2 blue strips of 78 cm x 8 cm and stitch onto the sides.

☐ Cut 2 blue strips of 92 cm x 8 cm and stitch onto the top and the bottom.

☐ Press the top on the reverse side.

Layers

☐ Cut a backing and the batting, each measuring 96 cm x 96 cm.

☐ Layer the backing, the batting and the top and baste (p. 6).

Note If you would like to use the quilting design above, first trace it onto the large off-white blocks before basting the 3 layers.

Quilting

☐ Quilt (p. 6-7) along the lines of the quilting design with a light-coloured thread.

☐ Use a dark-coloured thread to quilt diagonally across the dark blocks. Also quilt along the stitching lines between the 9 checked fabric blocks and the off-white blocks.

Binding

☐ Trim the edges.

☐ Cut a blue strip of 4 m x 5 cm and bind the quilt (p. 7-8).

Note The strip of binding may be joined.

Log cabin (photographs on p. 23)

The log cabin is one of the easiest and most popular of the traditional patchwork designs. This particular colour combination is called "Barn raising". Traditionally, the smallest middle block is red to represent a fireplace. By simply cutting wider strips, the same instructions can be used to make a quilt for a bed.

Measurements

☐ Size of quilt, 22 cm x 17 cm

☐ Size of middle block, 17,5 cm x 11,5 cm

☐ Size of each block, 4 cm x 4 cm

☐ Number of blocks, 24

☐ Width of borders, 0,5 cm and 1,5 cm respectively

Materials

☐ Several light- and dark-coloured remnants for blocks

☐ Red remnant for inner border and middle blocks

☐ Black print remnant for outer border

☐ Matching fabric for the backing, 26 cm

☐ Wine-red remnant for binding

☐ Thin batting, 26 cm x 20 cm

Assembling

Middle block

☐ Cut a number of light and dark strips of 2 cm wide and 24 red middle patches of 2 cm x 2 cm.

☐ Place a red square on a dark strip, stitch together to the end and cut off the dark strip along the edge of the red square. Each time before adding the next strip, trim the 6 mm seam allowance of each set to eliminate the bulky seams as you proceed.

☐ Press the seam to the left on the reverse side (away from red block).

☐ Place the red-dark set on a dark strip with right sides facing, stitch together and cut off the dark strip along the edge of the red-dark set.

☐ Place this square on a light strip with right sides facing, stitch and cut off (see top of p. 33).

☐ Continue by alternately sewing 2 dark and 2 light strips around the outer edge. Stop after the eighth strip.

 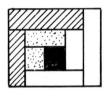

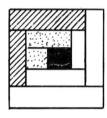

☐ Make 23 more blocks and press on the reverse sides.
☐ Arrange the blocks in 4 rows of 6 blocks each (see below), stitch together the blocks in each row and then stitch the rows together.

☐ Trim the 6 mm seam allowances and press the middle block.

African print in red and blue is an excellent choice and is typically South African. On the table is the *Furrows in the field* quilt (p. 34-35), on the floor to the right is the *Stripes* quilt (p. 14-15) and to the left is the *Attic window* quilt (p. 53-55).

Borders
☐ Cut 2 red strips according to the length of the vertical sides (± 18 cm) and 1,5 cm wide and stitch onto both sides of the completed middle block.
☐ Cut 2 red strips according to the length of the horizontal sides (including the red vertical borders) (± 13 cm) and 1,5 cm wide and stitch onto the bottom and the top.
☐ Cut 2 black print strips according to the length of the vertical sides (± 21 cm) and 3 cm wide and stitch onto both sides.
☐ Cut 2 black print strips according to the length of the horizontal sides (including the black vertical borders) (± 17 cm) and 3 cm wide and stitch

them onto the top and bottom.
☐ Press the completed top on the reverse side.

Layers
☐ Cut a backing and the batting, each measuring 26 cm x 21 cm.
☐ Layer the backing, the batting and the top and baste (p. 6).

Quilting
☐ Quilt (p. 6-7) around each of the 24 blocks.

Binding
☐ Trim the edges.
☐ Cut a wine-red strip of 90 cm x 2 cm and bind the quilt (p. 7-8).

Furrows in the field (photograph on p. 33)

The lines of this quilt are achieved by simply rearranging the ever-popular log cabin design. This particular design is one of the oldest from America and is often used by the Amish women in their beautiful quilts, especially because they can identify with the straight lines of ploughed fields.

This is a quick-cut, quick-stitch project. The red and various blue African prints are easily obtainable and blend well to create a typically African look. *Hint* Use the reverse side of the Africa print on the right side of the quilt to achieve a totally new colour effect.

Measurements
☐ Size of quilt, 95 cm x 70 cm (large enough for a knee-warmer)
☐ Size of middle block, 71 cm x 48 cm
☐ Width of borders, 2 cm and 8,5 cm respectively

Materials
☐ Red fabric for binding, inner border and centre blocks, 50 cm
☐ Light blue or white fabric, 50 cm
☐ Various dark blue African prints for strips, 50 cm
☐ Matching fabric for backing, 80 cm
☐ Medium blue African print for outer border and strips, 50 cm
☐ Thin batting, 100 cm x 76 cm

Assembling

Middle block
☐ Cut 1 red strip of 80 cm x 3 cm, 14 light blue or white strips of 80 cm x 3 cm and 18 blue strips of 80 cm x 3 cm.
☐ Place a red strip on a light blue strip with right sides facing and stitch from the right-hand side.

☐ Cut this strip set into 24 sets of 3 cm wide.

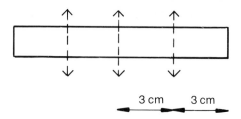

☐ Fold open the sets and press the seams in the direction of the dark fabric.

☐ Place one of the light blue 80 cm strips right side up on the sewing machine.
☐ Place a red-light blue set on the light blue strip, right sides facing, with the light blue block furthest away from you. Stitch together from the right-hand side to the end of the red block while you flatten the seam joining the red and light blue away from you.

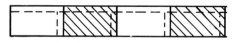

☐ Place the next red-light blue set against the previous one, again with the light blue block furthest away from you, and stitch.
☐ Continue like this until you have stitched 12 sets.
☐ Cut off what is left at the end of the light blue strip.
☐ Repeat with the next light blue strip and again stitch 12 sets onto the strip.
☐ Cut the strips between the sets into 24 units and fold open.

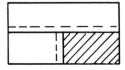

☐ Place one of the blue strips on the sewing machine right side up.
☐ Place one of the 24 units made above right side down, with the last colour that was added furthest from you, horizontally at the top of the blue strip. Stitch together in the same way as above.
☐ Add as many units as will fit onto the long blue strip.

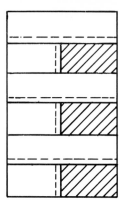

☐ Fold the block open.

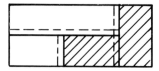

☐ Put another blue strip on the sewing machine with the right side up.
☐ Place a completed unit with the right side down and the last strip that was sewn on (blue) right at the top, horizontally on the long blue strip. Flatten the seams away from you as you sew (see below).

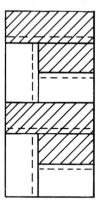

☐ Add units as described (± 8 units will go on a strip), cut off excess fabric, fold open and press.

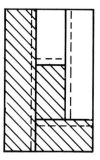

☐ Place a light strip on the sewing machine and continue stitching on units. Look at the photograph on p. 33 and notice that the dark blue strips are stitched on twice, in other words, each blue shade is used twice in succession. This means that 6 light and 6 dark strips are used on either side of the red square. There are 13 strips in all in each log cabin.

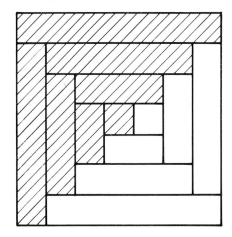

☐ Complete another 23 blocks and press.
☐ Arrange the blocks to form light and dark stripes (see below) and stitch the log cabins together in 6 rows of 4 each.

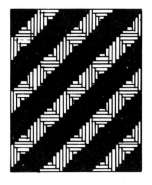

Note The log cabins may be arranged differently, for example as in *Log cabin* (photograph on p. 23).

Borders
☐ Cut 2 red strips of 75 cm x 3 cm and stitch onto both sides of middle block.
☐ Cut another 2 red strips of 54 cm x 3 cm and stitch onto the top and bottom.
☐ Cut 2 blue strips of 78 cm x 10 cm and stitch onto both sides of the middle block.

☐ Cut 2 blue strips of 71 cm x 10 cm and stitch onto the top and bottom.
☐ Press the seams sideways.

Layers
☐ Cut a backing and the batting, each measuring 108 cm x 76 cm.
☐ Layer the backing, the batting and the top and baste (p. 6).

Quilting
☐ Quilt (p. 6-7) along the stitching lines between the 24 log cabins.

Binding
☐ Trim the edges.
☐ Cut a red strip of 3,6 m x 5 cm and bind the quilt (p. 7-8).

Twenty-four stars (photograph below)

This bright quilt has many possibilities – it can feature as a wall-hanging, a tablecloth, a knee-warmer, or a cot cover. The stars are stitched in squares (which eliminates any difficult triangles) and are put together by the chain-piecing method. By following the step-by-step instructions you will gain valuable experience and discover a new world of sewing pleasure.

Measurements
☐ Size of quilt, 95 cm x 80 cm
☐ Size of middle block, 56 cm x 46 cm
☐ Width of borders, 4 cm each

The red and white *Twenty-four stars* quilt (p. 35-38) and the two *Trip around the world* quilts (variations of those on p. 43-45) are made according to the quick-cut, quick-stitch method.

Materials
☐ White fabric for middle block and borders, 1 m
☐ Red fabric for middle block and borders, 1,5 m
☐ Matching fabric for backing, 1 m
☐ Thin batting, 100 cm x 84 cm

Assembling
☐ Cut a white and a red block, each measuring 95 cm x 26 cm.
☐ Place the white block reverse side up on a table. Using an ordinary pencil, draw squares of 6,5 cm x 6,5 cm on the white block. There will be 12 horizontal and 4 vertical lines.

6,5 cm

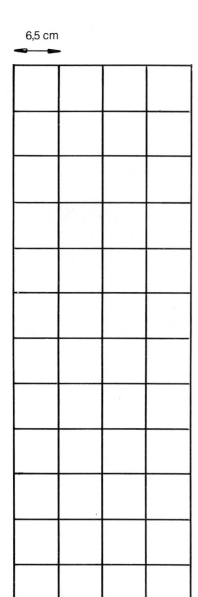

☐ Draw *diagonal* lines through the squares.

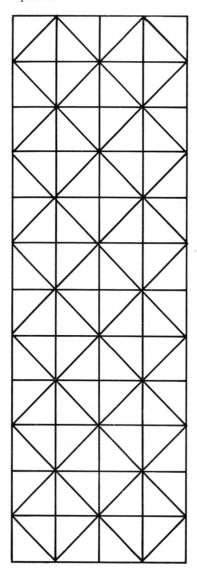

☐ Using a pencil or pen with water-soluble ink, draw dotted lines (to become 6 mm seam allowances) on both sides of each diagonal line (see diagram above right).

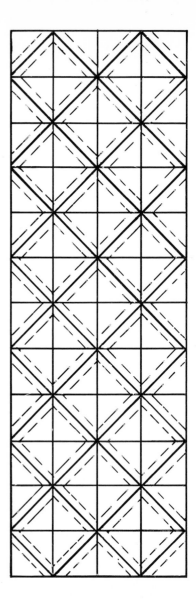

☐ Put the white block on the red block with right sides facing and pin together. Do not put the pins on or close to the lines.

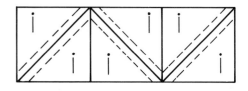

☐ Stitch along *all* the dotted lines.
☐ Press.
☐ Cut through all the solid lines – there will be 96 triangles.
☐ Fold open the triangles to give 48 squares.
☐ Press the white seams in the direction of the red ones.

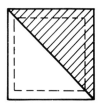

☐ Cut 5 white strips of 100 cm x 5 cm, stack them and cut into 100 squares of 5 cm x 5 cm.

Hint A rotary cutter will easily cut through all the layers simultaneously.

☐ Cut 24 red squares of 5 cm x 5 cm for the middle blocks.

☐ The 24 star blocks are easily assembled by stitching together 9 squares in 3 rows of 3 squares each. Take great care to arrange the triangles exactly as shown:

Row 1: white + red-and-white + white
Row 2: red-and-white + red + red-and-white
Row 3: white + red-and-white + white

Row 1

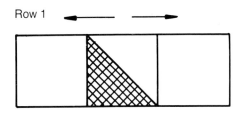

Row 2

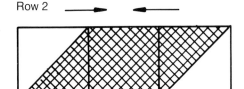

Row 3

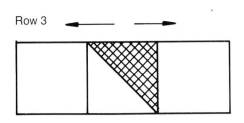

☐ Press the seam allowances in the direction of the arrows.
☐ Stitch the 3 rows together to form a star block.
☐ Stitch the completed star blocks together in 5 rows of 4 each to give 20 stars.

Note The 4 remaining stars are used on the corners of the border.

Borders
☐ Cut 2 red strips of 47 cm x 5 cm, 2 red strips of 57 cm x 5 cm, 4 white strips of 47 cm x 5 cm and 4 white strips of 57 cm x 5 cm.
☐ Stitch together a white, red and another white 47 cm strip and sew onto the one short side of the middle block. Repeat on the other side.
☐ Make 2 white-red-white 57 cm strips, stitch a star block onto both ends on the white block and stitch it onto the opposite long sides of the middle block (see facing page).
By now you should have an idea of what the end product will look like.
☐ Cut 2 red strips of 71,5 cm x 9 cm and 2 red strips of 95,5 cm x 9 cm.
☐ Stitch the red 71,5 cm strips onto the short sides of the middle block and the 95,5 cm strips onto the other 2 sides.
☐ Press the top.

Layers
☐ Cut a backing and the batting, each measuring 100 cm x 84 cm.
☐ Layer the backing, the batting and the top and baste (p. 6).

Quilting
☐ Quilt (p. 6-7) around the stars and along all the stitching lines.

Binding
☐ Trim the edges.
☐ Cut a red strip of 3,9 m x 5 cm and bind the quilt (p. 7-8).

Scalloped border (optional)
A scalloped border is an interesting variation:
☐ Make a template of the scallop (top of p. 38), place it with its narrowest part on the edge exactly above the middle star of the middle block and trace with a pencil.
☐ Mark the whole border – there should be 3 inlets on each side – and cut along the pencil marks.
☐ Cut a red bias strip of 4 m x 5 cm and bind the scalloped edge (p. 7-8).

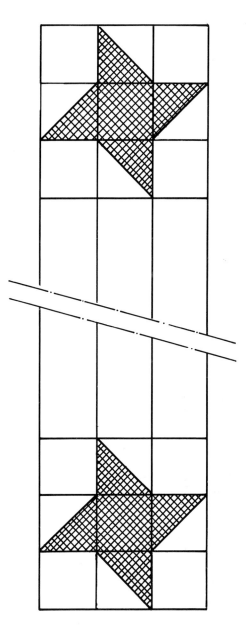

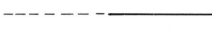

Star log cabin (photograph facing)

This quilt consists of nine log cabins, a wide three-strip border and stars in the corners. When you have finished this project, you will have mastered quite a number of basic techniques: the quick-cut, quick-stitch method, colour contrasts, the log cabin technique, stitching triangles without working with acute angles, assembling a quilt and quilting on your own. Is this not sufficient reason for making a spectacular quilt?

Measurements
☐ Size of quilt, 95 cm x 95 cm
☐ Size of each block, 17 cm x 17 cm
☐ Number of blocks, 9
☐ Width of borders, 7 cm each

Materials
☐ Off-white fabric for the 5 light-coloured log cabins and border, 1,5 m
☐ Light brown fabric for the light section of the 4 light-dark log cabins, 25 cm
☐ Brown fabric for the dark section of the 4 light-dark log cabins, border, binding and backing, 1,75 m
☐ Thin batting, 100 cm x 100 cm

If you think you can cope with learning the three techniques, i.e. the quick-cut, quick-stitch, the log cabin and the star techniques, all at once, then *Star log cabin* (p. 38) is just the project for you! The *Candlewicking* quilt in the foreground (p. 66) is the exact replica of her bigger sister: the traditional full-size bedspread. Behind is the *Framed cottage* quilt (p. 59-60).

Assembling

Light log cabins (make 5)

☐ Cut 2 off-white strips of 20 cm x 4 cm and 8 off-white strips of 110 cm x 4 cm.

☐ Stitch the 2 off-white 20 cm strips together with right sides facing. Do not fold open.

☐ Cut this double strip into 5 sets of 4 cm wide.

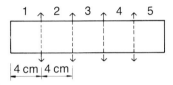

☐ Fold open and, with your fingers, press the seams down to one side.

☐ Number the sets 1, 2, 3, 4 and 5. One half of the set is A and the other half B.

☐ Place an off-white 110 cm strip on the sewing machine right side up and place set 1 horizontally and face down over this strip. Push the seam away from you as you pass over it while stitching slowly down the right-hand side.

☐ Place set 2 next to set 1 with A next to B and stitch.

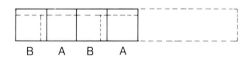

☐ Repeat with sets 3, 4 and 5. Remember to push each seam back, away from you.

☐ Cut off the rest of the 110 cm strip along the edge of set 5. (Take another look at the diagram above.)

☐ Divide the long strip into 5 units by cutting between sets 1 and 2, 2 and 3, 3 and 4, and 4 and 5. This is what such a unit will look like (C is the part of the long strip that was added).

☐ Place an off-white 110 cm strip on the sewing machine right side up. Place the first unit right side down over it with C in a horizontal position at the top.

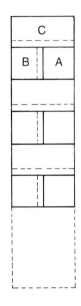

☐ Place the rest of the units on the strip next to one another and stitch to the end of set 5 while you once again push the seams back and away from you as you stitch.

☐ Cut off the rest of the long strip, cut between the units and fold open (the part that was added is D).

☐ Continue adding strips by this chain stitching method (up to M = 13 strips). The part that was added last will always be at the top of the block. Note that the block is rotated clockwise all the time. The completed block will be about 19 cm x 19 cm.

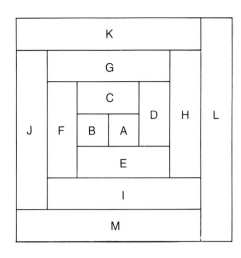

The 5 off-white log cabins have been completed. You made all of them at the same time! This is what is called *quick stitching*!

Light-dark log cabins (make 4)

☐ Cut 1 brown and 1 light brown strip of 16 cm x 4 cm, and 3 brown and 3 light brown strips of 110 cm x 4 cm.

☐ Stitch together a light brown and a brown 16 cm strip with right sides facing. Do not fold open.

☐ Cut this double strip into 4 sets of 4 cm wide.

☐ Fold the sets open and flatten the seams to one side with your finger.

☐ Number the sets 1, 2, 3 and 4.

☐ Place a light brown 110 cm strip on the sewing machine right side up and place set 1 horizontally on this strip with right side down. (The light brown section of set 1 should be furthest from you.) Stitch.

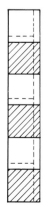

☐ Add all the sets in the same way.
Note The light brown strip is always at the top.

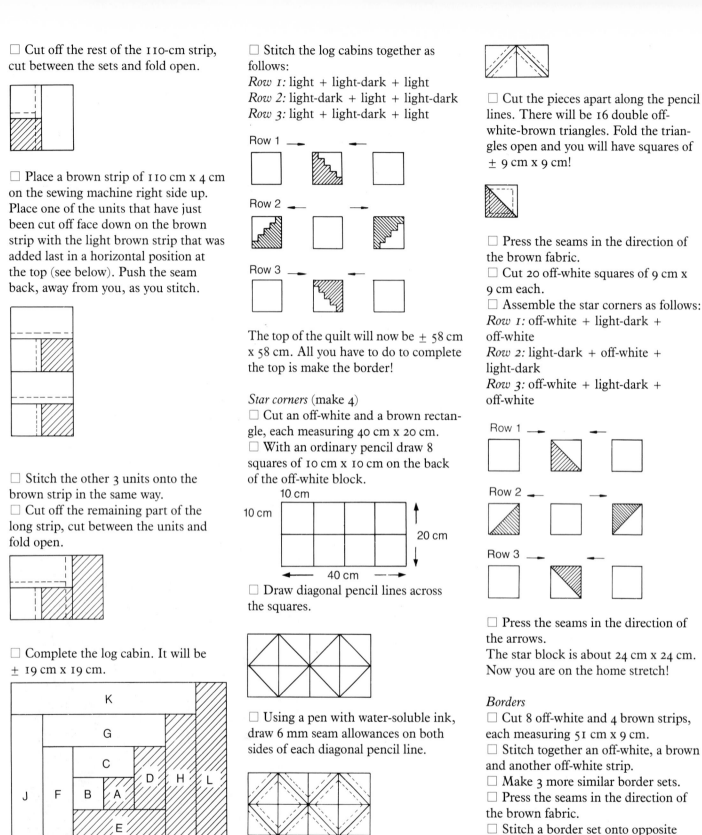

□ Cut off the rest of the 110-cm strip, cut between the sets and fold open.

□ Place a brown strip of 110 cm x 4 cm on the sewing machine right side up. Place one of the units that have just been cut off face down on the brown strip with the light brown strip that was added last in a horizontal position at the top (see below). Push the seam back, away from you, as you stitch.

□ Stitch the other 3 units onto the brown strip in the same way.
□ Cut off the remaining part of the long strip, cut between the units and fold open.

□ Complete the log cabin. It will be ± 19 cm x 19 cm.

□ Complete another 3 log cabins.

□ Stitch the log cabins together as follows:
Row 1: light + light-dark + light
Row 2: light-dark + light + light-dark
Row 3: light + light-dark + light

Row 1

Row 2

Row 3

The top of the quilt will now be ± 58 cm x 58 cm. All you have to do to complete the top is make the border!

Star corners (make 4)
□ Cut an off-white and a brown rectangle, each measuring 40 cm x 20 cm.
□ With an ordinary pencil draw 8 squares of 10 cm x 10 cm on the back of the off-white block.

□ Draw diagonal pencil lines across the squares.

□ Using a pen with water-soluble ink, draw 6 mm seam allowances on both sides of each diagonal pencil line.

□ Place the marked off-white block on the brown block with right sides together. Pin together, stitch along the ink lines and press.

□ Cut the pieces apart along the pencil lines. There will be 16 double off-white-brown triangles. Fold the triangles open and you will have squares of ± 9 cm x 9 cm!

□ Press the seams in the direction of the brown fabric.
□ Cut 20 off-white squares of 9 cm x 9 cm each.
□ Assemble the star corners as follows:
Row 1: off-white + light-dark + off-white
Row 2: light-dark + off-white + light-dark
Row 3: off-white + light-dark + off-white

Row 1

Row 2

Row 3

□ Press the seams in the direction of the arrows.
The star block is about 24 cm x 24 cm. Now you are on the home stretch!

Borders
□ Cut 8 off-white and 4 brown strips, each measuring 51 cm x 9 cm.
□ Stitch together an off-white, a brown and another off-white strip.
□ Make 3 more similar border sets.
□ Press the seams in the direction of the brown fabric.
□ Stitch a border set onto opposite sides of the top.
□ Stitch a star block onto both ends of each of the other 2 border sets (see above right). Stitch these 2 border sets onto the 2 open sides.
□ Press on the wrong side.
□ Pin the top to a drawn curtain and

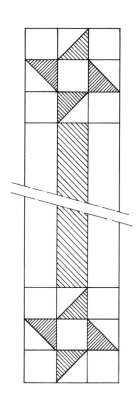

stand back to admire what you have achieved!
☐ If you prefer designs on the off-white blocks, trace them in pencil.

Layers
☐ Cut a brown backing and batting 100 cm x 100 cm.
☐ Layer the backing, the batting and the top and baste (p. 6).

Quilting
☐ Instead of designs, you could quilt (p. 6-7) along the stitching lines.

Binding
☐ Trim the edges.
☐ Cut a brown strip of 4 m x 5 cm and bind the quilt (p. 7-8).

Lightning (photograph on p. 31)

As quick as lightning – a few remnants in five shades (from light to dark) are turned into an attractive miniquilt.

Measurements
☐ Size, 50 cm x 40 cm

Materials
☐ Remnants in 5 different colours (dark, medium dark, medium, medium light and light), 15 cm each
☐ Matching fabric for backing, 50 cm
☐ Thin batting, 50 cm x 40 cm

Assembling
☐ Cut 4 strips of 60 cm x 3 cm in each of the 5 colours (altogether 20 strips).
☐ Stitch 5 strips together.

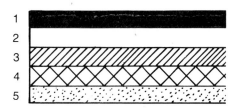

☐ Repeat 4 more times.
Note Number the colours from dark (1) to light (5).
☐ Cut each of the strip sets along the width into 20 sets of 3 cm wide.

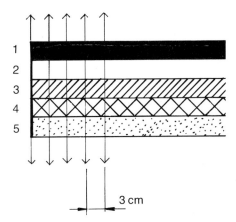

☐ Stitch together 5 of the sets (each set consists of 5 different coloured blocks) to form a long set of 25 blocks.
☐ Make another 19 long rows consisting of 25 blocks each.
☐ Stitch the 20 rows together (see below)

Any quilt can be framed to make an attractive wall-hanging. Here the *Trip around the world* (p. 43-45) and *Four-block* (p. 29) quilts are done mainly with strips, the latter being an excellent project for all those who have never made a quilt.

☐ The pattern takes shape automatically through the removal and adding of blocks. Row 1 remains unchanged. The top block is removed from row 2 and added to the bottom. The top 2 blocks of row 3 are removed as a unit and stitched to the bottom. Three blocks are removed from row 4 and 4 blocks from row 5.
☐ Stitch together the 20 rows in the same sequence as the separate rows.

Layers
☐ Cut a backing and the batting, each measuring 50 cm x 42 cm.
☐ Layer the backing, the batting and the top and baste (p. 6).

Quilting
☐ Quilt (p. 6-7) across every second diagonal row.
☐ Quilt along all the stitching lines.

Binding
☐ Trim the edges.
☐ Cut a dark strip of 2 m x 5 cm and bind the quilt (p. 7-8).

Trip around the world (photographs on pp. 35 and 42)

This is the ultimate practice quilt. Although the design looks complicated, if you follow the diagrams, the pattern falls into place as if by magic. The same technique can be applied for a large quilt or for something smaller such as a tablecloth, simply by adjusting the width of the strips. Once you understand this ridiculously simple technique (which dates back to the turn of the century), you are well on your way to making a large quilt for your bed. Just imagine the effect – a quilt on your bed with a smaller version on the wall!

The secret of this quilt lies in the use of fabrics in contrasting colours. Our quilt consists of maroon, navy blue, light blue, dark pink, pale pink, blue with white dots and white fabrics. Rely on your instinct for colour. If colours look right to *you*, they will form a good design. After all, no one else can tell you what you should like.

It is important, though, that you keep track of the seven colours while you work. Cut off a sample of each colour, arrange from light to dark, paste onto a piece of cardboard and number from 1 to 7. Keep this card at hand while you work and check regularly that your colours and numbers still match.

Measurements
☐ Size of quilt, 45 cm x 45 cm
☐ Size of middle block, 26 cm x 26 cm
☐ Size of each block, 2 cm x 2 cm
☐ Width of borders, 5 cm and 4 cm respectively

Materials (for quilt depicted on p. 42)
☐ 7 different light to dark fabrics, 20 cm each
☐ Wine-red and light pink prints for borders, 10 cm each
☐ Maroon fabric for binding, 10 cm
☐ Matching fabric for backing, 45 cm
☐ Thin batting, 50 cm x 50 cm

Assembling

Middle block
The middle block consists of 4 identical blocks (each consisting of 49 squares) arranged to form a pattern. Between the blocks are 4 single strips (of 7 squares each) with a single block in the centre.
☐ Cut a strip of ± 80 cm x 2,5 cm in each of the 7 colours.
☐ Stitch the 7 strips together along the long edges with a seam allowance of 3 mm. Notice how the light and dark colours are grouped together: the darkest colour is 2 and the lightest 6.

☐ Press the seams alternately towards and away from each other. If you do this they will not all fall together at intersections and the corners will not be pushed apart when they are being stitched.
☐ Cut the strips along the width in ± 32 sets of 2,5 cm wide each. Each of these sets consists of one block of each of the 7 colours.
☐ Place one of the sets (A) on a table. Take a second set (B), carefully unravel the first square (colour 1), place it next to colour 7 and stitch:

☐ From the third set (C), remove 2 squares (colours 1 and 2) as a unit and stitch onto colour 7:
☐ From the fourth set (D), remove the first 3 squares (colours 1-3) and stitch onto colour 7.

☐ Continue up to the seventh set (G).
☐ Stitch all the sets together. At each corner, make sure that the seams do not both lie in the same direction. You have now completed one of the large squares.

	A	B	C	D	E	F	G
A	1	2	3	4	5	6	7
B	2	3	4	5	6	7	1
C	3	4	5	6	7	1	2
D	4	5	6	7	1	2	3
E	5	6	7	1	2	3	4
F	6	7	1	2	3	4	5
G	7	1	2	3	4	5	6

☐ Make 3 more identical blocks.
☐ Press the 4 blocks.
☐ Place the 4 blocks on a table. Check the colours (numbers) against the diagram on p. 44.
☐ Place the 4 joining sets, each consisting of the 7 colours, between the 4 blocks.

□ Place a single block in colour 1 right in the centre (see diagram on p. 44).
□ Stitch the top left and right-hand blocks onto the upper vertical joining set.
□ Repeat with the lower blocks and the second vertical joining set.
□ Stitch the 2 sections onto the horizontal joining sets and the single centre block. The emerging design will make you feel very proud of yourself!

	A	B	C	D	E	F	G
A	1	2	3	4	5	6	7
B	2	3	4	5	6	7	1
C	3	4	5	6	7	1	2
D	4	5	6	7	1	2	3
E	5	6	7	1	2	3	4
F	6	7	1	2	3	4	5
G	7	1	2	3	4	5	6

1
2
3
4
5
6
7

	G	F	E	D	C	B	A
	7	6	5	4	3	2	1
	1	7	6	5	4	3	2
	2	1	7	6	5	4	3
	3	2	1	7	6	5	4
	4	3	2	1	7	6	5
	5	4	3	2	1	7	6
	6	5	4	3	2	1	7

1	2	3	4	5	6	7

1

7	6	5	4	3	2	1

G	7	1	2	3	4	5	6
F	6	7	1	2	3	4	5
E	5	6	7	1	2	3	4
D	4	5	6	7	1	2	3
C	3	4	5	6	7	1	2
B	2	3	4	5	6	7	1
A	1	2	3	4	5	6	7

7
6
5
4
3
2
1

6	5	4	3	2	1	7
5	4	3	2	1	7	6
4	3	2	1	7	6	5
3	2	1	7	6	5	4
2	1	7	6	5	4	3
1	7	6	5	4	3	2
7	6	5	4	3	2	1

□ Press the middle block carefully on the reverse side.

Borders
□ Measure the sides of the middle block – they should be the same length. If not, calculate the average length (p. 8).
□ Cut 2 light pink strips according to the length of the vertical sides (± 29,5 cm) and 6 cm wide and stitch onto both sides of the centre block. Press the seams outwards.
□ Cut 2 light pink strips according to

the length of the horizontal sides (including the vertical strips) and 6 cm wide and stitch onto the top and bottom. Press the seams outwards.
□ Repeat with the wine-red outer border, but cut strips of 5 cm wide.

Layers
□ Cut the backing and the batting ± 4 cm wider than the top all round (± 50 cm x 50 cm).

□ Layer the backing, the batting and the top and baste (p. 6).

Quilting
□ Quilt (p. 6-7) diagonally across each square.

Binding
□ Trim the edges.
□ Cut a maroon strip of 2 m x 4 cm and bind the quilt (p. 7-8).

Flower garden (photograph on p. 23)

Although this floral quilt looks complicated, it is actually quite simple to make. If you keep your wits about you with the six colours, the flowers in your garden will fall into place like the pieces of a jigsaw puzzle. The joy of this quilt is that the seams do not have to match. A flower out of line here and there will add to the charm of the quilt!

Measurements
□ Size of quilt, 44 cm x 36 cm
□ Width of strips, 2,5 cm

Materials
□ Remnants (6 colours, including a fair amount of leaf-green) for blocks, ± 10 cm x 10 cm each
□ Brown fabric for the border, 15 cm
□ Light green fabric for binding, 15 cm
□ Matching fabric for backing, 50 cm
□ Thin batting, 50 cm x 40 cm

Assembling
It is a good idea to stick a sample of each colour onto a piece of cardboard next to its colour symbol. This will prevent you from becoming confused.

Middle block
□ Cut at least 3 strips at a time of each of the 6 colours, each measuring 20 cm x 2,5 cm. (You may cut more later if necessary.)
□ Stitch the strips together in groups of 3. Follow the diagrams to combine the colours correctly. There should be 9 strips of 3 different colour combinations. Press all the seams in the same direction.

Strip 1   Strip 2

Strip 3

Strip 4

Strip 5

Strip 6

Strip 7

Strip 8

Strip 9

☐ Cut a single leaf-green strip of 20 cm x 2,5 cm.

☐ Cut the different strips across in sets of 2 cm.

☐ Place the different colour combinations in separate piles – there should be 10.

Note One pile will consist only of single leaf-green blocks.

☐ Row 1: Stitch the different colour combinations together in vertical rows, in other words, start with set 5 and join to set 7. Follow up with sets 5, 6, 5, 7, 5. Row 1 on the left side has now been completed (see below).

☐ Row 2: Begin with set 3.

Note Half of the top green patch protrudes above the first row – it will be trimmed later.

☐ Add another set 3 and then set 4, etc.

☐ Stitch the vertical rows together.

Note The seams do not match up – each seam should be roughly opposite the centre of the adjoining patch.

☐ Press the completed top first on the reverse side and then on the right side.

Layers

☐ Cut a backing and the batting, each measuring 50 cm x 40 cm.

☐ Layer the backing, the batting and the top and baste (p. 6).

Quilting

☐ Using green thread, quilt (p. 6-7) around the "flowers" to accentuate them.

Borders

☐ Cut 2 brown strips according to the length of the vertical sides (± 40 cm) and 2,5 cm wide and stitch onto both sides.

☐ Cut 2 brown strips according to the length of the horizontal sides (± 35 cm) and 2,5 cm wide and stitch onto the top and bottom.

Binding

☐ Trim the edges (also the protruding leaf-green blocks) of the quilt.

☐ Cut a light green strip of ± 170 cm x 6 cm and bind the quilt (p. 7-8).

Row 1 2 3 4 5 6 7 8 9 10 11 12 13 14 15 16 17

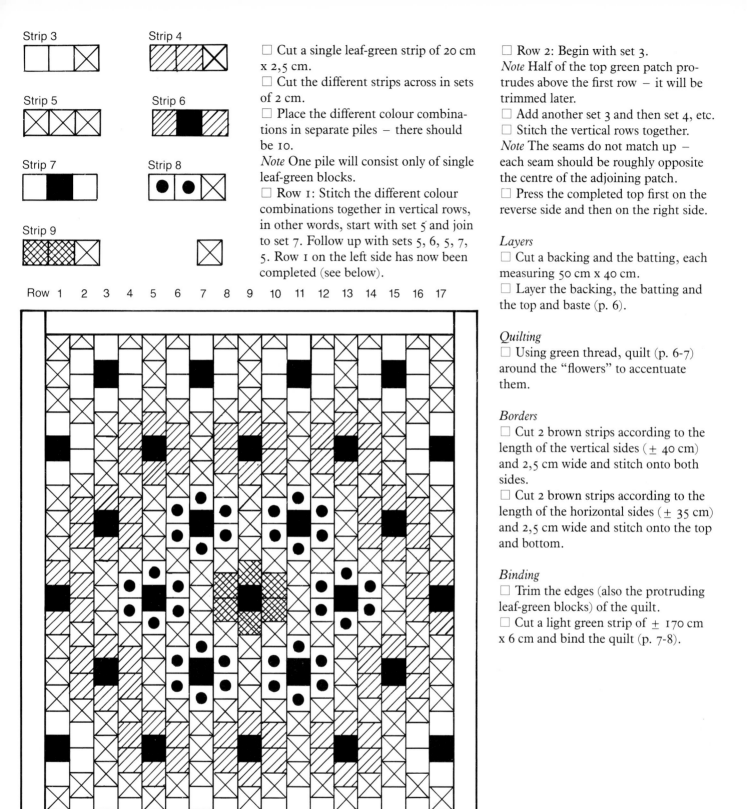

Charms (photograph on p. 28)

This quilt with its "charming" appearance will certainly be an eye-catcher. Use any colour and any fabric for the small hearts – cotton, polyester, silk or wool. Cut small heart shapes out of your children's cast-off clothes to make a remembrance quilt which you will cherish in years to come. Sew these shapes onto the patches with blanket stitch. Make twenty-five hearts (see photograph), or if time is precious, make only four to form a small wall-hanging. Even a single heart turned into a pincushion will be very effective.

Measurements
☐ Size of quilt, 50 cm x 50 cm
☐ Size of middle block, 35 cm x 35 cm
☐ Size of each block, 7 cm x 7 cm
☐ Number of blocks, 25
☐ Width of blue border, 7 cm

Materials
☐ 25 different remnants
☐ Off-white fabric for background, 50 cm
☐ Blue fabric for borders, 25 cm
☐ Yellow fabric for binding, 10 cm
☐ Matching fabric for backing, 60 cm
☐ Thin batting, 60 cm x 60 cm
☐ Black DMC embroidery thread

Assembling

Middle block
☐ Cut 25 off-white squares of 9 cm x 9 cm each.

☐ Make a heart-shaped template (below), trace it onto the remnants and cut out 25 hearts.
☐ Pin a heart onto each square.
☐ Using 3 threads of black embroidery thread and large blanket stitching, sew on the hearts.

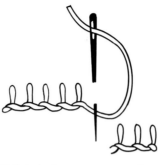

☐ Stitch the squares together in 5 rows of 5 squares each and then join the 5 rows.
☐ Press the middle block.

Border
☐ Cut 2 blue strips according to the length of the vertical sides (± 35 cm) and 9 cm wide and stitch onto both sides of the middle block.
☐ Cut 2 blue strips according to the length of the horizontal sides (including the vertical blue strips) (± 50 cm) and 9 cm wide and stitch onto the top and bottom.
☐ Press the completed top on the reverse side.
☐ Trace the heart design given above onto the blue border to give 7 hearts on each of the vertical borders and 5 on each of the horizontal borders.

Layers
☐ Cut a backing and the batting, each measuring 60 cm x 60 cm.
☐ Layer the backing, the batting and the top and baste (p. 6).

Quilting
☐ Quilt (p. 6-7) along the outlines of the hearts and also along all the stitching lines.

Binding
☐ Trim the edges.
☐ Cut a yellow strip of 2,1 m x 5 cm and bind the quilt (p. 7-8).

Nine hearts (photograph on p. 28)

In contrast to the 25 hearts in different colours which are appliquéd in black blanket stitch, the hearts on this quilt are sewn on by the more familiar method, which makes it an ideal project for beginners! The 3 mm seam allowance is folded under and the heart sewn on with invisible slip stitches. The border consists of four strips and creates an interesting finish. The echo quilting around the hearts creates a unique effect.

Measurements
☐ Size of quilt, 48 cm x 48 cm
☐ Size of middle block, 33 cm x 33 cm
☐ Size of each block, 11,5 cm x 11,5 cm
☐ Width of borders, 2 cm each

Materials
☐ Off-white print fabric for blocks, 2 borders and backing, 75 cm
☐ Brown-blue print fabric for hearts, squares for third border and binding, 25 cm
☐ Blue fabric for inner border, 10 cm
☐ Remnants for third border
☐ Thin batting, 52 cm x 52 cm

Assembling

Middle block
☐ Cut 9 off-white print squares of 12 cm x 12 cm each.
☐ Make a template of the heart design (above right), trace the outline onto brown-blue print and cut out 9 hearts.
☐ Appliqué one heart on each of the 9 squares by hand (p. 7-8).
☐ Stitch together 3 rows of 3 squares each and stitch the 3 rows together.
☐ Press the middle block carefully on the reverse side (do not press the seams open).

Borders
☐ Cut 2 blue strips according to the length of the vertical sides (± 36 cm) and 3 cm wide and stitch onto both sides of the middle block.
☐ Cut 2 blue strips according to the length of the horizontal sides (± 37 cm) and 3 cm wide and stitch onto the top and bottom.

☐ Press the seams away from the middle block.
☐ Cut 2 off-white print strips according to the length of the vertical sides (including the blue borders) (± 38 cm) and 3 cm wide and stitch onto both sides.
☐ Cut 2 off-white print strips according to the length of the horizontal sides (including the blue borders) (± 41 cm) and stitch onto the top and bottom.
☐ Cut any number of 3 cm strips of remnants. Stitch together.
Hint Try to alternate light and dark strips.
☐ Press all the seams in the same direction.
☐ Cut the strips across into sets of 3 cm wide.
☐ Measure the top and bottom sides of the middle block (± 42 cm).
☐ Stitch the patchwork strips onto the top and bottom.
Note You will probably have to add or take away a few small squares to reach the desired length.
☐ Measure the left and right sides (± 44,5 cm).
☐ Stitch patchwork strips onto the 2 sides. Once again you will have to add or remove small squares to reach the required length.
☐ Cut 2 off-white print strips according to the length of the vertical sides (± 48 cm) and 3 cm wide and stitch onto both sides.

☐ Cut 2 off-white print strips according to the length of the horizontal (± 45 cm) and 3 cm wide and stitch onto the top and bottom.
☐ Press all the border seams away from the middle block.
☐ Draw triple quilting lines around each heart, 6 mm apart.

Layers
☐ Cut an off-white print backing and the batting, each measuring 52 cm x 52 cm.
☐ Layer the backing, the batting and the top and baste (p. 6).

Quilting
☐ Quilt (p. 6-7) along three lines drawn (5 mm apart) around each heart (this is called echo quilting).
☐ Quilt along the stitching lines between the 9 squares.
☐ The quilting lines of the border are 2 cm apart (the width of the patchwork squares of the third border). Quilt along the stitching lines of the patchwork border and continue quilting in both directions across the second border and inner border up to the edge of the middle block, and across the outer border to the outer edge of the quilt.

Binding
☐ Cut a brown-blue print strip of 2 m x 5 cm and bind the quilt (p. 7-8).

Fanned heart (photograph on p. 49)

Make this romantic tablecloth (or wall-hanging) in soft, hazy hearts today and learn the technique of shadow quilting at the same time. The technique consists of pasting the different parts of the fans onto the background and covering them with voile or any other see-through fabric. Finally each patch is quilted along the edge to keep it in position. There are no seams, therefore this is the ideal project for someone who is wary of patchwork but does not mind cutting, pasting and sewing a few straight stitches!

Measurements
☐ Size of quilt, 53 cm x 50 cm
☐ Size of middle block, 40 cm x 38 cm
☐ Width of border, 4 cm

Materials
☐ Light pink fabric for background, 50 cm
☐ Dark pink fabric for fan, 20 cm
☐ Blue and light pink remnants for fan
☐ White voile, 50 cm
☐ Matching fabric for backing, 60 cm
☐ Thin batting, 60 cm x 55 cm
☐ Lace, 4 cm wide, 2 m

Assembling

Middle block
☐ Cut a light pink rectangle of 42 cm x 40 cm (background).
☐ Make a template of the complete fan (p. 48), trace the outline onto the dark pink fabric and cut out 8 fans.
☐ Make a template of the panel (p. 48), trace the outline onto the pink and blue remnants and cut out 24 panels.
☐ Paste 2 or 3 blue and pink panels (alternate the colours) onto each fan, leaving 2 or 3 panel-sized openings between them so that the dark pink is visible as alternating panels.
☐ Arrange the 8 fans in the middle of the background to form a heart (p. 48).
☐ Trace the quilting heart design in the centre of and immediately above the fanned heart, and trace the other quilting design in the 4 corners of the background fabric.

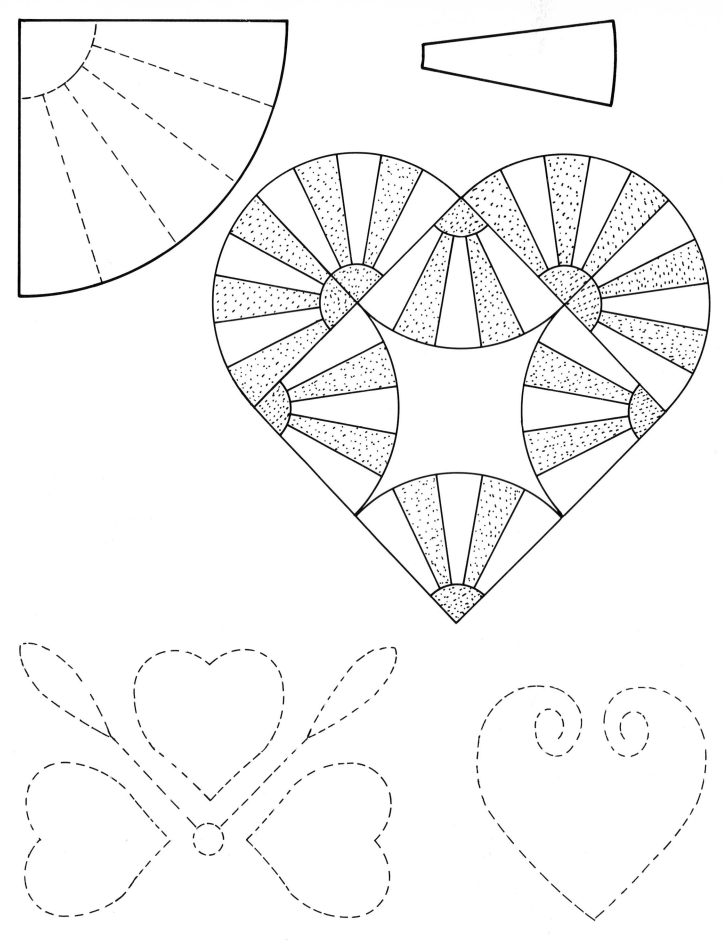

Layers

☐ Cut voile of 42 cm x 40 cm, place it over the heart and the background and pin down.
☐ Cut a backing and the batting, each measuring 60 cm x 55 cm.
☐ Layer the backing, the batting and the top and baste (p. 6).

Quilting

☐ Using red embroidery thread, quilt (p. 6-7) around the fanned heart, along the traced hearts in the centre of and above the fanned heart, around the designs at the corners, around the fans themselves and also between the panels of the fans.

Borders

☐ Trim the edges.
☐ Cut 4 dark pink strips of 40 cm x 5 cm and 4 strips of 50 cm x 5 cm.
☐ Take a pair of equal strips at a time and place them right sides and raw edges together with a strip of lace in between. Stitch along the raw edge, fold open and press.
☐ Stitch one edge of a 50 cm strip onto each side of the middle block and the two 40 cm strips onto the top and bottom.
☐ Fold the free edges of the unstitched pink strips in 6 mm at the back and hem with small stitches.

Fans (photograph on p. 51)

What could be more attractive than twelve pale pink and blue fans decorated with ribbons and lace? As a wall-hanging in a teenager's room or framed on the bathroom wall – somewhere you will find the right spot for this quilt to come into its own. This is also the perfect quilt to introduce beginners to the magic of patchwork.

Measurements

☐ Size of quilt, 60 cm x 50 cm
☐ Size of middle block, 42 cm x 31 cm
☐ Size of each square, 11 cm x 11 cm
☐ Width of borders, 3 cm and 7 cm respectively

Materials

☐ 7 different blue and pink fabrics, 12 cm each
☐ Blue fabric for borders and binding, 25 cm

The hazy *Fanned heart* quilt (p. 47-49) is made according to the shadow-appliqué method which requires very little stitching. There are endless possibilities for *Lady* (p. 60-62): try changing her hairstyle or decorate the dress with embroidery or lace.

☐ White-spotted fabric for background, border and backing, 1 m
☐ Thin batting, 64 cm x 54 cm
☐ Gathered lace 3 cm wide, 2 m
☐ Narrow blue ribbon, 3 m

Assembling

Middle block
☐ Cut 12 white-spotted squares of 13 cm x 13 cm.
☐ Make a template of the panels of the fan (see below), trace the outlines onto the blue and pink fabric and cut 3 pink and 3 blue panels for each of the 12 fans (6 x 12 = 72 panels).

☐ Make a template of the corner of the fan, trace the outline onto the blue fabric and cut out 12 corners.

☐ Stitch together 3 blue panels, 3 pink panels and a blue corner as follows:

☐ Make 11 more fans.
☐ Place a fan in the bottom left-hand corner of each white-spotted square and fold the outside edge of the fan under.
☐ For each fan cut a 14 cm length of lace, fold it under the outside edge, baste and stitch the lace, together with the fan, onto the background square.
☐ Arrange the squares with fans in 4 rows of 3 squares each. First stitch 3 squares together horizontally and then stitch the 4 rows together.

Borders
☐ Cut 2 blue strips of 48 cm x 3 cm and stitch onto both sides of the middle block.
☐ Cut 2 blue strips of 34 cm x 3 cm and stitch onto the top and bottom.
☐ Cut 2 white-spotted strips of 60 cm x 7 cm and stitch onto both sides.
☐ Cut 2 white-spotted strips of 37 cm x 7 cm and stitch onto the top and bottom.

☐ Press the top.
☐ Trace the quilting design (below) along the border.

Layers
☐ Cut a backing and the batting, each measuring 64 cm x 54 cm.
☐ Layer the backing, the batting and the top and baste (p. 6).

Quilting
☐ Quilt (p. 6-7) around the design, along the edges of each fan and around each square.
☐ Quilt along the stitching lines between the blue and the white-spotted borders.

Binding
☐ Trim the edges.
☐ Cut a blue strip of 2,4 m x 5 cm and bind the quilt (p. 7-8).
☐ Cut the blue ribbon in 12 pieces of equal length. Tie a bow and sew to the corner of each fan.

Fans always evoke a romantic mood, especially if you decorate them with ribbon and lace as in the photograph. A *Fan* quilt (p. 49-51) like this will look good in any room – even the bathroom! The panels of the different fans are cut out separately, stitched together and then worked onto a square. There are very few curves which would require special skills.

Scottish terriers

You will go a long way to find anything cuter than a miniquilt of six Scottish terriers, decorated in tartan and quilted in checks. The dogs are hand-appliquéd, but machine-work will be equally effective.

Measurements
☐ Size of quilt, 50 cm x 40 cm
☐ Size of middle block, 35 cm x 25 cm
☐ Size of each block, 12,5 cm x 12,5 cm
☐ Number of blocks, 6
☐ Width of border, 6,5 cm

Materials
☐ Off-white fabric for middle block, 25 cm
☐ 6 different checked fabric remnants for the dogs
☐ Checked fabric for the borders, 25 cm
☐ White or red fabric for the backing, 45 cm
☐ Black fabric for the binding, 10 cm
☐ Thin batting, 55 cm x 45 cm

Assembling

Middle block
☐ Cut 6 off-white blocks of 14,5 cm x 13,5 cm.
☐ Make a template of the dog, trace the outline onto the tartan remnants and cut out 6 dogs.
☐ Pin each dog into position on an off-white block and appliqué by hand or by machine (p. 5-6).
Note If you use the machine, do not leave a seam allowance.
☐ Stitch the blocks together in pairs along the short edges and then join the horizontal sides so that you end up with 3 rows of 2 dogs each.

Borders
☐ Cut 2 checked fabric strips according to the length of the vertical sides and 8 cm wide and stitch onto both sides of the middle block.
☐ Cut 2 checked fabric strips according to the length of the horizontal sides and 8 cm wide and stitch onto the top and bottom.
☐ Press the top.

52

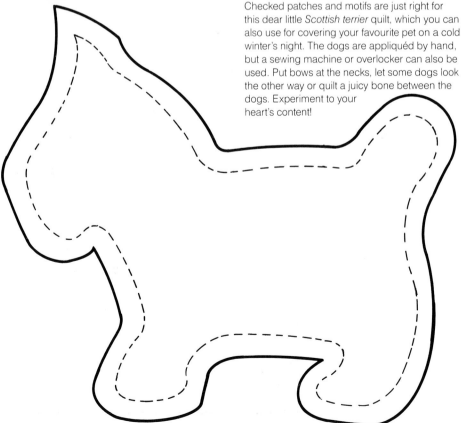

Checked patches and motifs are just right for this dear little *Scottish terrier* quilt, which you can also use for covering your favourite pet on a cold winter's night. The dogs are appliquéd by hand, but a sewing machine or overlocker can also be used. Put bows at the necks, let some dogs look the other way or quilt a juicy bone between the dogs. Experiment to your heart's content!

☐ Draw 2 diagonal lines 6 mm apart across the middle block and the next line 2 cm further to give a double line alternated by a single line.

Layers
☐ Cut a backing and the batting, each measuring 55 cm x 45 cm.
☐ Layer the backing, the batting and the top and baste (p. 6).

Quilting
☐ Quilt (p. 6-7) on the diagonal lines and around the middle block.

Binding
☐ Cut a black strip according to the length and width of the quilt and 6 cm wide and bind the quilt (p. 7-8).

Attic windows (photograph on p. 54)

The attic window technique is very simple, and it is one of the most striking projects described in this book. The uninitiated should try to use this technique for a first quilt – if only to experience the satisfaction of achieving something unique.

The technique consists of stitching together only three different colours, which creates the illusion of windows. There are hundreds of possibilities, for example a garden scene of which only parts are visible through a window. The photograph on p. 56 gives an idea of the scope that animals offer. You could even depict a fairy tale like Little Red Riding Hood from the first window to the last. Give your imagination free reign.

Measurements
☐ Size of quilt, 70 cm x 70 cm
☐ Size of middle block, 54 cm x 54 cm
☐ Size of each window block, 16 cm x 16 cm
☐ Number of window blocks, 9
☐ Width of borders, 1,5 cm and 7 cm respectively

Materials
☐ Navy blue fabric for window blocks, 85 cm
☐ Red fabric for window edges, 85 cm
☐ Striped fabric for windowsill, 85 cm
☐ Light blue fabric for lattice strips, 50 cm
☐ White fabric for backing, 75 cm
☐ Thin batting, 75 cm x 75 cm

Assembling

Middle block
☐ Cut 9 navy blue window squares (template A below), 9 red window edges (template B on p. 54) and 9 striped windowsills (template C on p. 54).

A

☐ Stitch the red window edges onto one side of each blue window.

☐ Stitch a striped windowsill to the bottom of each window.

Hint To make a perfect corner where templates B and C meet, pin the red window edge onto the window. Stitch from the outside up to 6 mm from the corner. Stitch one stitch backwards. Do not cut the thread. Lift the presser foot, lift the needle, turn the fabric in the new direction, lift the needle over the seam, lower it into the fabric, stitch one stitch backwards, then stitch to the end.

☐ Press the seams to one side.

☐ Make 8 more windows.

☐ Cut 9 light blue strips of 17 cm x 3 cm and 3 light blue strips of 58 cm x 3 cm.

☐ Arrange the 9 windows in 3 rows of 3 windows each. Place the 17 cm x 3 cm strips below the windows and stitch together (see diagram on p. 55).

The middle block of the *Attic window* quilt seen close-up. The contrast between the fabrics lends an extra dimension to the quilt to give the effect of looking through the window.

B

C

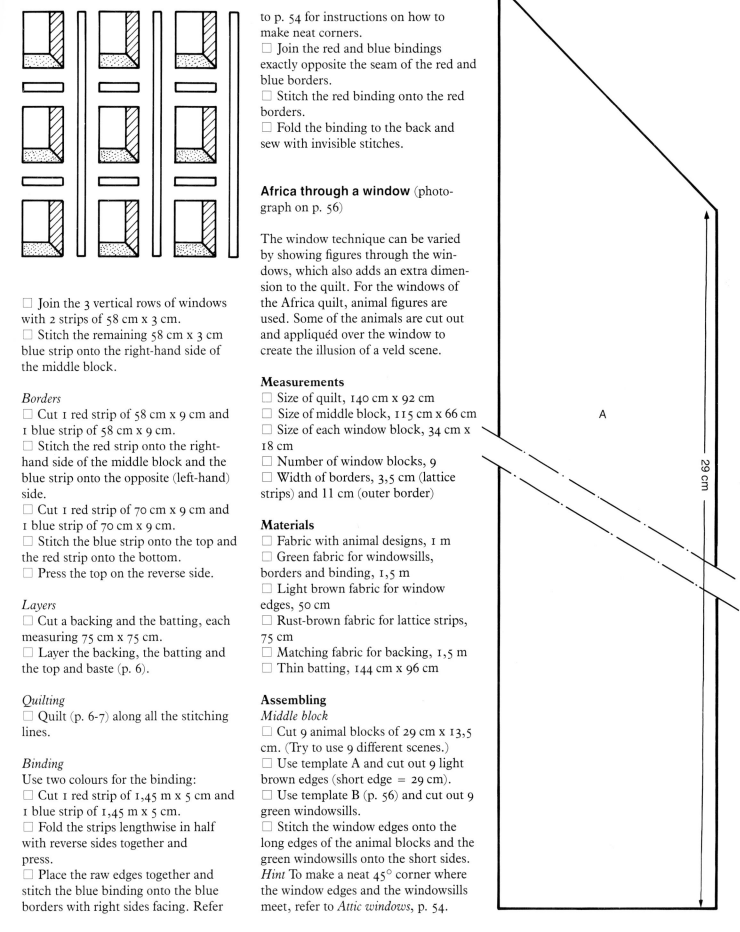

□ Join the 3 vertical rows of windows with 2 strips of 58 cm x 3 cm.
□ Stitch the remaining 58 cm x 3 cm blue strip onto the right-hand side of the middle block.

Borders
□ Cut 1 red strip of 58 cm x 9 cm and 1 blue strip of 58 cm x 9 cm.
□ Stitch the red strip onto the right-hand side of the middle block and the blue strip onto the opposite (left-hand) side.
□ Cut 1 red strip of 70 cm x 9 cm and 1 blue strip of 70 cm x 9 cm.
□ Stitch the blue strip onto the top and the red strip onto the bottom.
□ Press the top on the reverse side.

Layers
□ Cut a backing and the batting, each measuring 75 cm x 75 cm.
□ Layer the backing, the batting and the top and baste (p. 6).

Quilting
□ Quilt (p. 6-7) along all the stitching lines.

Binding
Use two colours for the binding:
□ Cut 1 red strip of 1,45 m x 5 cm and 1 blue strip of 1,45 m x 5 cm.
□ Fold the strips lengthwise in half with reverse sides together and press.
□ Place the raw edges together and stitch the blue binding onto the blue borders with right sides facing. Refer

to p. 54 for instructions on how to make neat corners.
□ Join the red and blue bindings exactly opposite the seam of the red and blue borders.
□ Stitch the red binding onto the red borders.
□ Fold the binding to the back and sew with invisible stitches.

Africa through a window (photograph on p. 56)

The window technique can be varied by showing figures through the windows, which also adds an extra dimension to the quilt. For the windows of the Africa quilt, animal figures are used. Some of the animals are cut out and appliquéd over the window to create the illusion of a veld scene.

Measurements
□ Size of quilt, 140 cm x 92 cm
□ Size of middle block, 115 cm x 66 cm
□ Size of each window block, 34 cm x 18 cm
□ Number of window blocks, 9
□ Width of borders, 3,5 cm (lattice strips) and 11 cm (outer border)

Materials
□ Fabric with animal designs, 1 m
□ Green fabric for windowsills, borders and binding, 1,5 m
□ Light brown fabric for window edges, 50 cm
□ Rust-brown fabric for lattice strips, 75 cm
□ Matching fabric for backing, 1,5 m
□ Thin batting, 144 cm x 96 cm

Assembling
Middle block
□ Cut 9 animal blocks of 29 cm x 13,5 cm. (Try to use 9 different scenes.)
□ Use template A and cut out 9 light brown edges (short edge = 29 cm).
□ Use template B (p. 56) and cut out 9 green windowsills.
□ Stitch the window edges onto the long edges of the animal blocks and the green windowsills onto the short sides.
Hint To make a neat 45° corner where the window edges and the windowsills meet, refer to *Attic windows*, p. 54.

This *Africa through a window* quilt (p. 55-57) brings the countryside into your home! Simply use the basic Attic window method (p. 53-55) with a little appliqué work. The possibilities of this method are infinite.

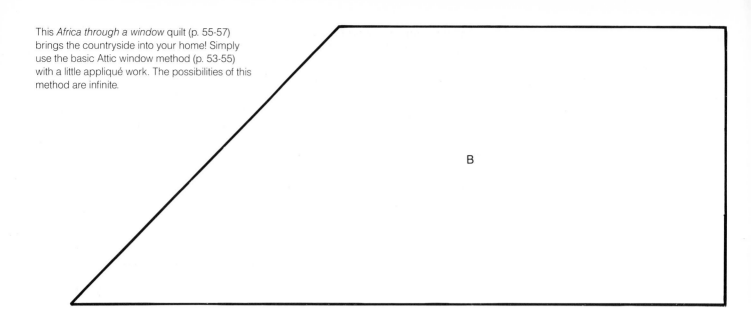

B

☐ Cut 9 light brown strips of 19 cm x 4,5 cm and 4 light brown strips of 114 cm x 4,5 cm.
☐ Arrange the 9 window blocks in 3 rows of 3 windows each (photograph facing).
☐ Stitch the short light brown strips to the bottoms of the window blocks.
☐ Stitch together the 3 blocks of each vertical row.
☐ Stitch 2 long light brown strips between the vertical rows to join them, and stitch the remaining 2 onto the outsides.
☐ Press the completed middle block.

Borders
☐ Cut 2 green strips of 118 cm x 13 cm and stitch onto both sides of the middle block.
☐ Cut 2 green strips of 92 cm x 13 cm and stitch onto the top and bottom.
☐ Press the top.

Appliqué
☐ Cut out animal designs similar to those used in the windows. Include a seam allowance around the design.
☐ Place these cut-out designs over part of similar designs on the quilt (see photograph).
Hint Change the position of the animals by lowering, for example, the neck of the giraffe.
☐ Fold in the seam allowance and appliqué by hand (p. 5) the design onto the background with invisible stitches.

Layers
☐ Cut a backing and the batting, each measuring 144 cm x 96 cm.
☐ Layer the backing, the batting and the top and baste (p. 6).

Quilting
☐ Quilt (p. 6-7) around the animal designs you want to accentuate, as well as along the stitching lines and around the windows and borders.

Binding
☐ Trim the edges.
☐ Cut a green strip of 5 m x 6 cm and bind the quilt (p. 7-8).

Cottages (photograph on p. 11)

Patchwork cottages have always been a popular project. The cottages look attractive anywhere – in the kitchen, the entrance hall, children's room, on the front door or even in a classroom. A single cottage might decorate a pot-holder or be framed, while a quilt with 24 cottages will cover a single bed. There is scope for playing around with embroidered chimney-smoke, trees, flowers or clouds, or with lace curtains in the windows. Numbers or the letters of the alphabet embroidered along the borders are another possibility.

The cottages are made by stitching on the different parts, or by sewing them on by hand. Start off with one cottage to become familiar with the design. Even though the quick-cut, quick-stitch method is not used for this project, it will give as much pleasure as the other quilts.

Measurements
☐ Size of quilt, 78 cm x 57 cm
☐ Size of middle block, 71 cm x 49 cm
☐ Size of each cottage block, 16 cm x 16 cm
☐ Number of cottage blocks, 6
☐ Width of border, 3 cm

Materials
☐ Navy blue print for cottages and binding, 30 cm
☐ Wine-red fabric for roofs, chimneys and doors, 25 cm
☐ Yellow remnants for windows
☐ Navy blue checked fabric for borders and binding, 50 cm
☐ Off-white fabric for background and backing, 1 m
☐ Thin batting, 82 cm x 61 cm

Assembling

Middle block
☐ Make templates of the 8 parts of the house (below and on p. 58).

☐ Trace the outlines onto the fabric and cut out the following parts for each cottage:
A = 1 off-white
B = 4 navy blue print
C = 1 yellow, 3 navy blue print, 1 off-white and 1 wine-red
D = 1 navy blue print
E = 1 wine-red
F = 2 off-white
G = 1 wine-red
H = 1 navy blue print

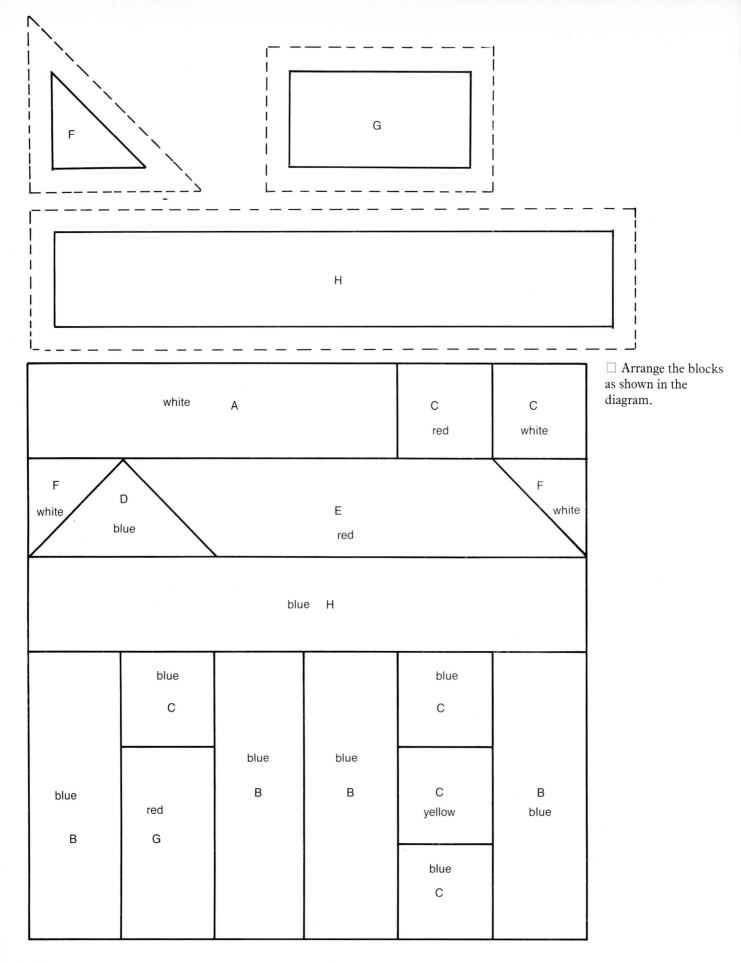

□ Arrange the blocks as shown in the diagram.

58

☐ Each cottage is stitched together in 4 strips. Start with the bottom strip.
☐ Stitch a blue C onto the red G, and a blue C onto both sides of the yellow C. Together with the 3 B's you will now have equal-sized blocks for the bottom strip.
☐ Stitch the 6 blocks together as follows: blue B, blue-red C-G, blue B, blue B, blue-yellow-blue C-C-C, blue B.
☐ Stitch the blue H onto the completed bottom strip.
☐ Make the roof by stitching together F, D, E and F.
☐ Stitch the roof onto the blue H.
☐ Make the top strip by stitching together an off-white A, a red C and an off-white C.
☐ Stitch the top strip to the roof.
☐ Make 5 more cottages – each one should be 16,5 cm x 16,5 cm.
☐ Carefully press each cottage block on the reverse side.
☐ Cut 12 off-white strips of 16,5 cm x 4 cm and stitch onto the top and bottom of each of the 6 cottage blocks.
☐ Cut 12 off-white strips of 21 cm x 4 cm and stitch onto both sides of each cottage block.
☐ Press the seams.
☐ Cut 17 checked fabric strips of 21 cm x 5 cm and 12 off-white squares of 5 cm x 5 cm.
☐ Stitch the 6 cottages together as follows in 3 rows of 2 cottages each: checked fabric strip, cottage, checked fabric strip, cottage, checked fabric strip.
☐ Repeat twice.
☐ Stitch the 4 horizontal strips together as follows: off-white square, checked fabric strip, off-white square, checked fabric strip, off-white square.
☐ Repeat 3 more times.
☐ Stitch a horizontal strip onto the top and bottom of the first row of cottages. Stitch another row of cottages onto the second horizontal strip.
☐ Continue by alternately sewing on cottages and strips.
☐ Carefully press the middle block on the reverse side.

Borders
☐ Cut 2 off-white strips according to the length of the vertical sides ($\pm$ 72 cm)

and 5 cm wide and stitch onto both sides of the middle block.
☐ Cut 2 off-white strips according to the length of the horizontal sides ($\pm$ 50 cm) x 5 cm wide and stitch onto the top and bottom.
☐ Press the top.

Layers
☐ Cut an off-white backing and the batting, each measuring 82 cm x 61 cm.
☐ Layer the backing, the batting and the top and baste (p. 6).

Quilting
☐ Quilt (p. 6-7) around the windows and doors, along the outlines of the cottages and also along all the stitching lines of the strips and borders.
☐ Quilt horizontal and vertical lines across the middle of the windows to represent windowpanes.

Binding
☐ Trim the edges.
☐ Cut a blue checked fabric strip of 3,5 m x 5 cm and bind the quilt (p. 7-8).

Framed cottage (photograph on p. 38)

Use the remnants from one of your projects to make a framed quilt. The cottage is a very simple project, while the little lady (p. 60) requires a little more experience. Just imagine how attractive the framed cottage would look with one of your miniquilts! It could of course also be turned into a wall-hanging, a small tablecloth or a quilt. Stitch a few identical designs together and it becomes a quilt.

Measurements
☐ Size, 25,5 cm x 20,5 cm

Materials
☐ Mustard yellow, brown and beige remnants for the house and the backing
☐ Black fabric for the background, 16 cm
☐ Light green remnant for the border
☐ Thin batting, 27 cm x 22 cm
☐ Cardboard
☐ Wooden frame, 27 cm x 22 cm

Assembling

Middle block
☐ Make templates of the cottage, door, window and chimney (see p. 60).
☐ Trace the outlines of the cottage onto mustard yellow, the door and chimney onto brown and the window onto beige fabric. Cut out all the pieces.
☐ Cut out a black square of 15,5 cm x 15,5 cm for the background.
☐ Use a glue stick to paste the chimney in position on the background.
☐ Place the cottage in position on the chimney and appliqué the cottage.
☐ Paste the windows and the door onto the cottage and appliqué.
☐ With dark brown thread, machine-stitch horizontal and vertical lines across the windows to form windowpanes.

Border
☐ Cut 2 light green strips of 30,5 cm x 9 cm and stitch onto both sides of the house.
☐ Cut 2 light green strips of 16,5 cm x 9 cm and stitch onto the top and bottom.

Layers
☐ Cut a backing and the batting slightly larger than the top.
☐ Layer the backing, the batting and the top and baste (p. 6).

Quilting
☐ Quilt (p. 6-7) along the inner edges of the windows, the door, the roof and the chimney and along the stitching lines of the border.

Finishing (frame)
☐ Cut out a piece of cardboard of 25,5 cm x 20,5 cm.
☐ Place the quilt on the cardboard, fold back the edges and fasten at the back with masking tape.
☐ Put the quilt inside the frame and follow the manufacturer's instructions to complete.

Lady (photograph on p. 49)

Measurements
☐ Size, 26 cm x 17 cm

Materials
☐ Fabric for background
☐ Light blue, pink, off-white and blue remnants for lady, border and backing
☐ Wool for hair
☐ Thin batting, 30 cm x 20 cm
☐ Narrow blue ribbon
☐ Thin wooden board for back, 26 cm x 17 cm

Assembling

Middle block
☐ Make templates of the different parts of the lady (see below).
☐ Trace the outlines of the dress onto light blue, the heart and background onto pink and the head, arms and legs onto off-white fabric. Add a 6 mm seam allowance except for the head and heart which are machine-appliquéd. Cut out all the pieces.
☐ Appliqué the head onto the centre of the upper background section.
☐ Sew the lady together into 4 rows as follows:

Row 1: Stitch the arms onto the background sections.
Row 2: Appliqué the heart onto the centre of the bodice of the dress and stitch the arms onto the bodice.
Row 3: Stitch the dress onto both sides of the background.
Row 4: Stitch the legs onto the 3 lower background sections.
☐ Press the 4 rows.
☐ Stitch the rows together in the correct order and press again.

Borders
☐ Cut 2 blue strips of 25,5 cm x 6 cm and stitch onto sides of middle block.

61

☐ Cut 2 blue strips of 22 cm x 6 cm and stitch onto the top and bottom of the middle block.
☐ Press the seams towards the outside.
☐ Embroider eyes (French knots) and a V-shaped mouth (2 long stitches).
☐ Paste the hair on, tie with a narrow ribbon and form a bow.

Layers
☐ Cut the backing and the batting slightly larger than the top.
☐ Layer the backing, the batting and the top and baste (p. 6).

Quilting
☐ Quilt (p. 6-7) around the lady and along the stitching lines of the borders.

Finishing
☐ Place the quilt on the cardboard, fold back the edges and tape down with masking tape.

Bouquet (photograph on p. 23)

In your free moments you might like to embroider this small bouquet in red thread. Then follow the instructions for a patchwork border while you master the quick-cut, quick-stitch method at the same time.

Measurements
☐ Size of quilt, 24 cm x 24 cm
☐ Size of embroidered middle block, 19 cm x 19 cm
☐ Width of each border, 3 cm

Materials
☐ Off-white fabric for middle block and border, 30 cm
☐ Red fabric for border and binding, 30 cm
☐ Fabric for backing, 28 cm x 28 cm
☐ Thin batting, 28 cm x 28 cm
☐ Red embroidery thread
☐ Embroidery frame

Assembling

Middle block
☐ Cut an off-white square of 25 cm x 25 cm (or bigger if you are using a larger embroidery frame).
☐ Trace the bouquet design onto the off-white square and embroider in candlewicking stitches.
Note Follow the symbols for stitches and instructions in Alma Schwabe's *Candlewicking* and *Candlewicking designs* (Tafelberg Publishers).
☐ Wash the block first in cold and then in hot water and press on the reverse side.
☐ Trim the square to measure 20 cm x 20 cm.

Borders
☐ Cut 1 off-white and 1 red strip of 60 cm x 2 cm, join the long edges and press the seam in the direction of the red fabric.

☐ Cut the double strip along the width into sets of 6 cm.
☐ Make 2 borders for the vertical sides by stitching together 15 blocks for each border (see photograph on p. 23). Press carefully.
☐ Stitch the borders onto both sides of the middle block.
☐ Make 2 borders for the horizontal sides by stitching together 17 blocks for each side. Make sure there is a red block at the beginning and end of each strip.
☐ Stitch the borders onto the top and bottom.
☐ Cut 2 red strips according to the length of the vertical sides (± 21 cm) and 2 cm wide, stitch onto both sides of the middle block and press.
☐ Cut 2 red strips according to the length of the horizontal sides (± 23,5 cm) and 2 cm wide, stitch onto the top and bottom and press.

Layers
☐ Cut a backing and the batting, each measuring 38 cm x 28 cm.
☐ Layer the backing, the batting and the top and baste (p. 6).

Quilting
☐ Quilt (p. 6-7) around the embroidered bouquet to accentuate it, and also along all the stitching lines of the borders.

Binding
☐ Trim the edges.
☐ Cut a red strip of 100 cm x 3 cm and bind the quilt (p. 7-8).

Friendship

The idea of a quilt as a gift for a friend who is moving, an expectant mother or a favourite chum has become very popular. Compared with an expensive and time-consuming large quilt, this charming miniquilt costs next to nothing. The little hearts can be appliquéd, or embroidered in different candlewicking stitches. The names may be written by hand with permanent ink, or they may be embroidered.

Win the heart of many a friend by making this darling *Friendship* quilt (instructions below)!

Measurements
☐ Size of quilt, 32 cm x 25 cm
☐ Size of middle block, 27 cm x 21 cm
☐ Size of each square, 6 cm x 6 cm
☐ Number of blocks, 12
☐ Width of border, 2 cm

Materials
☐ Off-white fabric for the middle block and the backing, 40 cm each
☐ Green, red, 2 different shades of red prints, ± 10 cm each
☐ Dark green fabric for binding, 15 cm
☐ Thin batting, 30 cm x 34 cm
☐ Red embroidery thread

Assembling

Middle block
☐ Draw vertical and horizontal lines 6 cm apart on the 24 cm x 18 cm off-white fabric to give 12 squares.
☐ Make a template of the heart design and trace the outline onto 6 of these squares.

☐ Using 3 strands of red embroidery thread together, embroider the outlines as well as the inside parts of the hearts in different stitches (e.g. stem stitch, French knots and chain stitch).
☐ Cut out the squares with the embroidered hearts.
☐ Cut red, green and red print strips 2 cm wide.
☐ From the strips of the 2 red prints, cut 48 shorter 6 cm strips.
☐ From the red and green strips cut 48 squares of 2 cm x 2 cm.
☐ Stitch red print strips to both sides of the empty off-white blocks.

☐ Stitch red and green squares to both sides of the red print strips. Alternate the red and green squares (see photograph on p. 63).

☐ Arrange the squares in 4 rows of 3 squares each. Alternate embroidered squares with blank squares (see below). Stitch the 4 rows together. Note that a square consisting of 4 small squares is formed every 6 cm.
☐ Press the middle block.

Border
☐ Cut 2 green strips according to the length of the vertical sides (± 28 cm) and 2,5 cm wide and stitch onto both sides.
☐ Cut 2 green strips according to the length of the horizontal sides (including borders) (± 26 cm) and 2,5 cm wide and stitch onto the top and bottom.
☐ Press the top.

Layers
☐ Cut the off-white backing according to the size of the top, adding 2 cm all round (± 36 cm x 30 cm).
☐ Cut thin batting of ± 36 cm x 30 cm.
☐ Write the names of 6 people on the 6 blank off-white squares.
☐ Layer the backing, the batting and the top and baste (p. 6).

Quilting
☐ Quilt (p. 6-7) along all the stitching lines.

Binding
☐ Trim the edges.
☐ Cut a dark green strip of ± 120 cm x 4 cm and bind the completed quilt (p. 7-8).

Christmas decorations (photograph on p. 23)

Try something new for Christmas – decorations in shadow quilting appliqué! Once you have finished your first decoration and mastered the simple technique, the others will follow quickly. The only requirements are bright colours and a sharp pair of scissors.

Measurements
☐ Size of *Yacht, Broken star, Serrated star, Wild goose* and *Firtree* quilt, 10 cm x 10 cm
☐ Size of *Sunbonnet child*, 8 cm x 8 cm

Materials
☐ Off-white fabric for background, 10 cm
☐ Red and green fabric for designs and backing, 10 cm each
☐ Narrow red ribbon, ± 3,5 m
☐ Voile, 10 cm
☐ Red and green embroidery thread
☐ Thin batting

Assembling
☐ Cut off-white squares of 10 cm x 10 cm (8 cm x 8 cm for *Sunbonnet child*).
☐ Make templates of all the parts of the basic designs (below and on facing page), trace the outlines onto the red, green and off-white fabrics and cut out.

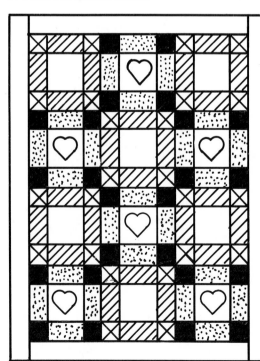

| Red | Off-white | Green |

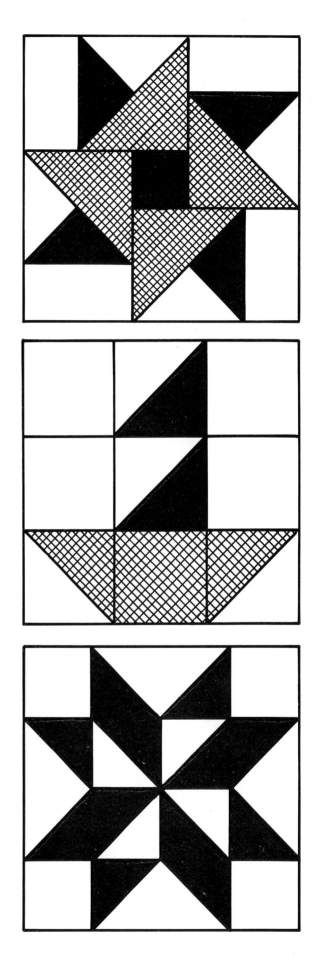

Hint Iron Vilene onto the back of the fabric before you start cutting.

☐ Use a glue stick to paste the sections of the designs onto the off-white squares according to the diagrams.

Layers

☐ Cut voile and batting squares slightly larger than the off-white background.

☐ Cut a red or green backing 1,5 cm wider than the background all round.

☐ Layer the backing, the batting, the background with the design and finally the voile, and baste (p. 6).

Quilting

☐ Quilt (p. 6-7) around each part of the designs with regular green or red machine thread.

"Binding"

☐ Fold the back of the quilt to the top and fold in the edge to form a "binding" of about 1 cm.

☐ Baste the "binding" and stitch onto the voile with small slip stitches.

Finishing

☐ On the voile, embroider French knots or stem stitches if desired.

☐ Cut off 25 cm of red ribbon, fold in half and stitch onto the back of one corner of the quilt. If the quilt cannot be hung by one corner, sew ribbons onto opposite corners, for example the *Firtree*.

☐ Cut off 15 cm of red ribbon, make a bow and sew onto 1 or 2 corners.

☐ Press the quilts and hang on the Christmas tree.

Candlewicking quilt (photograph on p. 38)

Sew a traditional off-white miniature candlewicking quilt and watch passionate lovers of candlewicking catch their breath! The designs are as old-fashioned as can be and only the basic candlewicking stitches have been used. This miniquilt is made in exactly the same way as the larger version. It is ideal for a young girl to practise basic candlewicking. It also makes a beautiful baby's pram cover.

A close-up of the middle block and strips of the *Candlewicking* quilt (instructions below). It is embroidered, assembled and quilted in exactly the same way as the large bedspread – but everything is done on a smaller scale.

Measurements

☐ Size of quilt, 100 cm x 75 cm

☐ Size of middle block, 84 cm x 61 cm

☐ Size of each block, 18 cm x 18 cm (the blocks must be cut big enough to fit in an embroidery frame)

☐ Number of blocks, 12

☐ Width of strips around blocks, 3 cm

☐ Width of strips between blocks, 5 cm

Materials

☐ Off-white fabric, 2 m

☐ Thin batting, ± 110 cm x 85 cm

☐ Lace (3 cm wide), 10 m

☐ Crotchet yarn or embroidery thread, no. 8

☐ Quilting thread

☐ Embroidery frame, 20 cm in diameter

Assembling

Middle block

☐ Cut 12 squares of 20 cm x 20 cm (or larger if you do not have a small embroidery frame and have to use a larger one).

☐ Trace the designs (p. 68-79) onto them. Embroider colonial knot, stem, chain, fishbone and satin stitch.

Note For candlewicking techniques follow the symbols for stitches and instructions in Alma Schwabe's *Candlewicking* and *Candlewicking designs* (Tafelberg Publishers).

☐ Wash the embroidered squares in cold water and then dip in very hot water. The tracing lines will disappear and the hot water will crease and slightly shrink the fabric. The embroidery thread also shrinks so that the knots stand out higher. Let the squares dry and press on the reverse side over a towel.

☐ Trim all the squares to measure 16 cm x 16 cm.

☐ Cut a strip of ± 10 m x 3 cm (the width of the lace). (If your lace is not 3 cm wide it does not matter. Simply cut the strips according to the width of the lace.) At this stage your quilt can be slightly bigger or smaller.

☐ Cut 24 strips of fabric and 24 lengths of lace of 16 cm x 3 cm.

☐ Baste the lace onto the strips of fabric.

☐ Place the strips on the left and right

sides of the embroidered squares with right sides facing, stitch and press to the outside

☐ Measure the horizontal sides, including the lace edges (± 20 cm).

☐ Cut 24 strips of fabric and 24 lengths of lace of 20 cm x 3 cm.

☐ Baste the lace onto the strips of fabric.

☐ Place the strips of fabric along the top and bottom of each block with right sides together, stitch and press outward. Take care that the seams are under the strips of lace.

☐ Cut 9 strips of 20 cm (length of the top strip of lace) x 5 cm.

☐ Arrange the embroidered blocks in 3 vertical rows of 4 blocks each.

☐ Stitch the strips horizontally onto the top of 9 embroidered blocks. Press the seams in the direction of the lace strips.

☐ Stitch together each row of 4 blocks.

☐ Cut 2 strips of 84 cm x 6 cm for the vertical sides.

☐ Stitch the 3 rows of blocks with their lattice strips onto one of the vertical strips and the next row of blocks onto this strip. Repeat between the other 2 rows of blocks.

Note First pin the blocks together and check that they are in line.

Borders

☐ Cut 2 strips according to the length of the vertical sides (± 83 cm) and 8 cm

wide and stitch onto both sides. Press the seams to the inside (underneath the lace strips).

☐ Cut 2 strips according to the length of the horizontal sides (including the 2 vertical sides) (± 75 cm) and 8 cm wide and stitch onto the top and bottom. Press the seams to the inside.

☐ Trace the quilting designs (p. 80) onto the strips and borders.

Layers

☐ Cut a backing and the batting, each measuring 110 cm x 85 cm.

☐ Layer the backing, the batting and the top and baste (p. 6).

Quilting

☐ Quilt (p. 6-7) around each candle-wicking design, between all the blocks and all along the border.

Binding

☐ Trim the edges.

☐ Cut 2 strips of 100 cm x 5 cm for the vertical sides and 2 strips of 75 cm x 5 cm for the horizontal sides and bind the quilt (p. 7-8).

Note As with most of the other projects, you could alternately make a continuous strip without seams at the corners. In that case, simply cut a strip of ± 3,75 m x 5 cm and use as binding.

☐ Wash the quilt to remove all tracing marks.

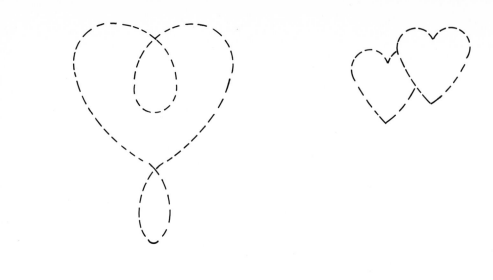

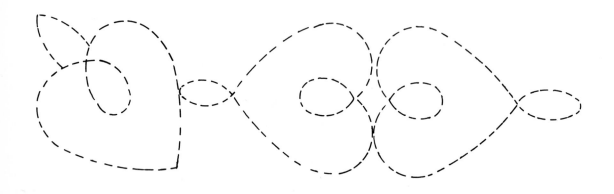

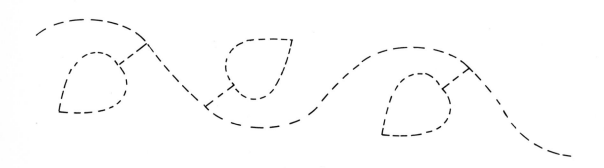